No Man Is a Desert Island

A Collection of Cartoons by

Felipe Galindo Feggo

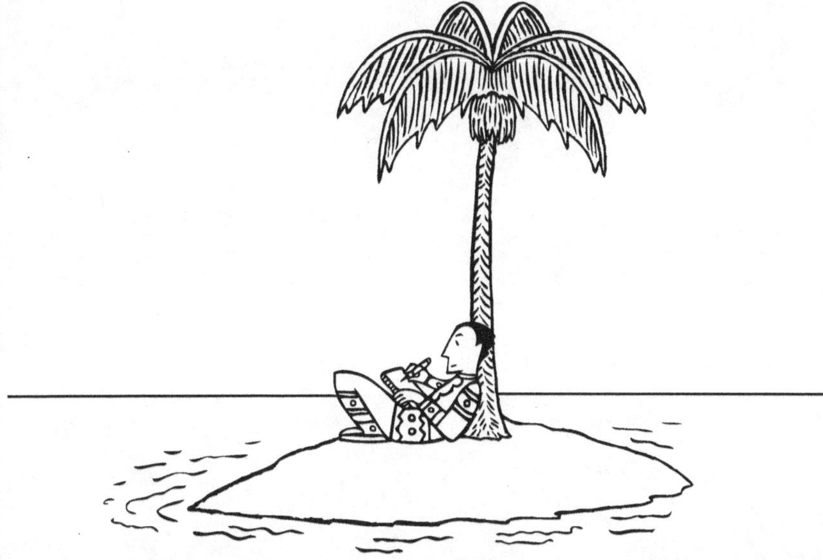

No Man Is a Desert Island

A Collection of Cartoons by

Felipe Galindo Feggo

Foreword by Sid Harris

Jorge Pinto Books Inc.
New York

No Man Is a Desert Island
A Collection of Cartoons by Felipe Galindo Feggo

Published by Jorge Pinto Books Inc. 2012
www.pintobooks.com

ISBN-13: 978-1-934978-69-6
ISBN-10: 1-934978-69-8

Foreword

by Sidney Harris

If you think it's easy to come up with an idea for a cartoon without a caption – after all, it's just someone doing something outlandish, or some unusual event happening – just try to think up about one thousand of them. There might be something funny about a firefly or King Arthur's Round Table or a jockey. But what? If you approach these problems the way Felipe Galindo does, you'll always come up with something surprising and unexpected. Who would think that a cartoon with a cow and a frog could ever make any sense, but the one here certainly does. You'll find in these pages the logical extension of those giant Easter Island heads, and the amazing idea of a funeral for a tree.

Galindo is never mean-spirited, never trying to show you that his wisecrack is one that you wish you had thought of. As a trained artist, he thinks visually, and doesn't have to rely on a one-liner or an insult – standard devices that many cartoonists regularly resort to.

His drawings have appeared in numerous periodicals, including *The New Yorker, Reader's Digest, Mad* and *National Lampoon*, and, because he is bilingual, bicultural and multi-talented (his paintings and collages would make another wonderful collection), in publications in Mexico, England, Holland, Switzerland, Japan, Austria and Germany.

As you might guess, Feggo is simply the pen name of Felipe Galindo Gómez. The letters are all in there, extracted and compressed, just the way his ideas extract and compress familiar events and objects in a truly distinctive and humorous manner.

P.S. Is there anything funnier than his 'Mayo Clinic' cartoon?

Sidney Harris is America's foremost science cartoonist and the author of more than twenty cartoon books including *Einstein Simplified* and *What's So Funny About Science.* Sidney's cartoons have appeared in numerous publications worldwide including *The New Yorker, American Scientist, The Wall Street Journal, Harvard Business,* and *Science.*

No Man Is a Desert Island

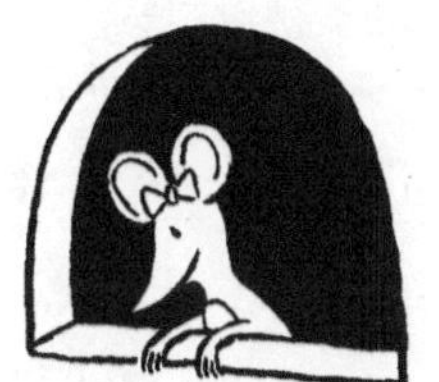

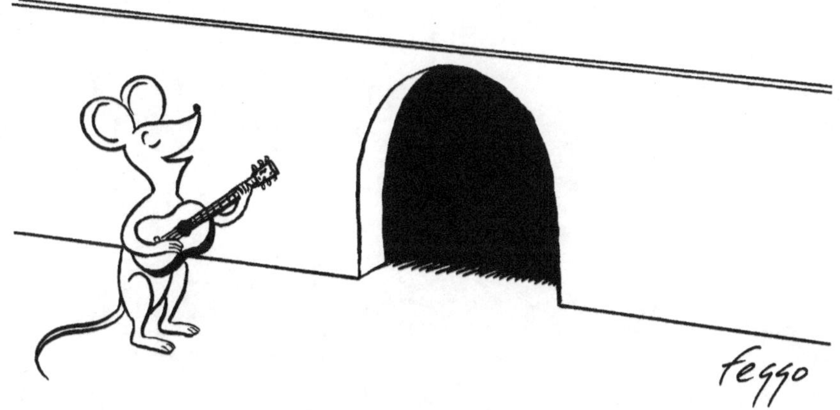

feggo

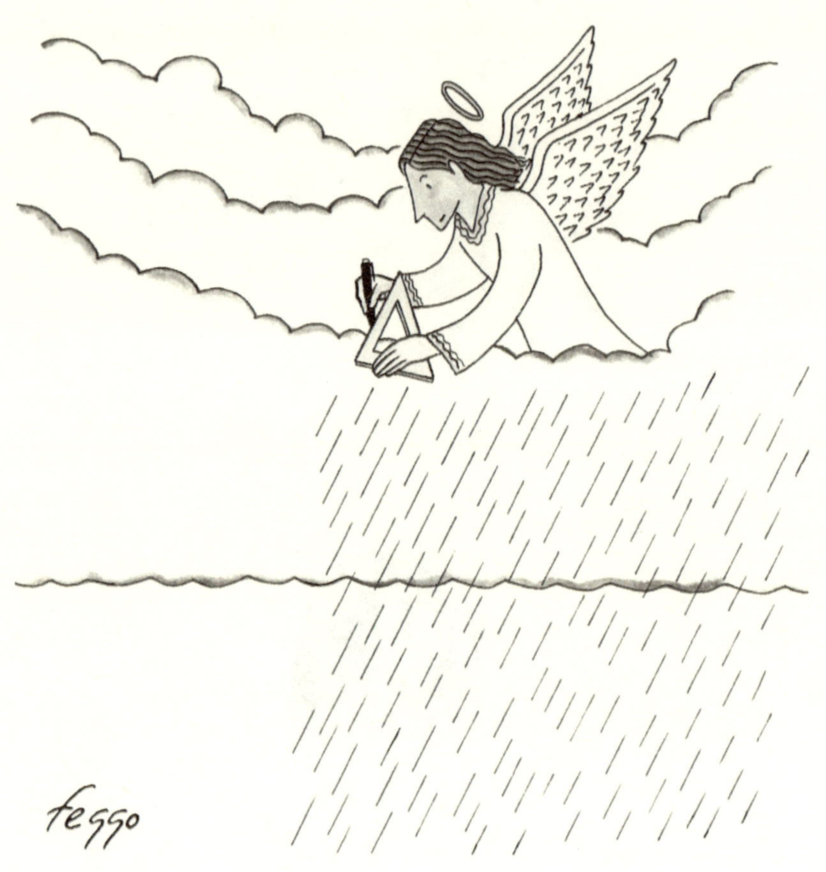
feggo

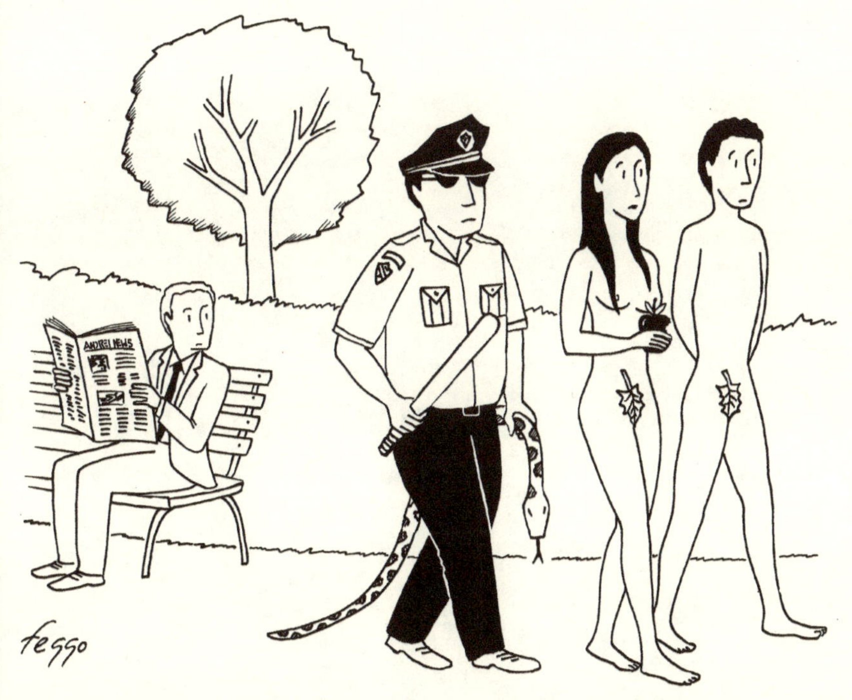
ANDREI NEWS
feggo

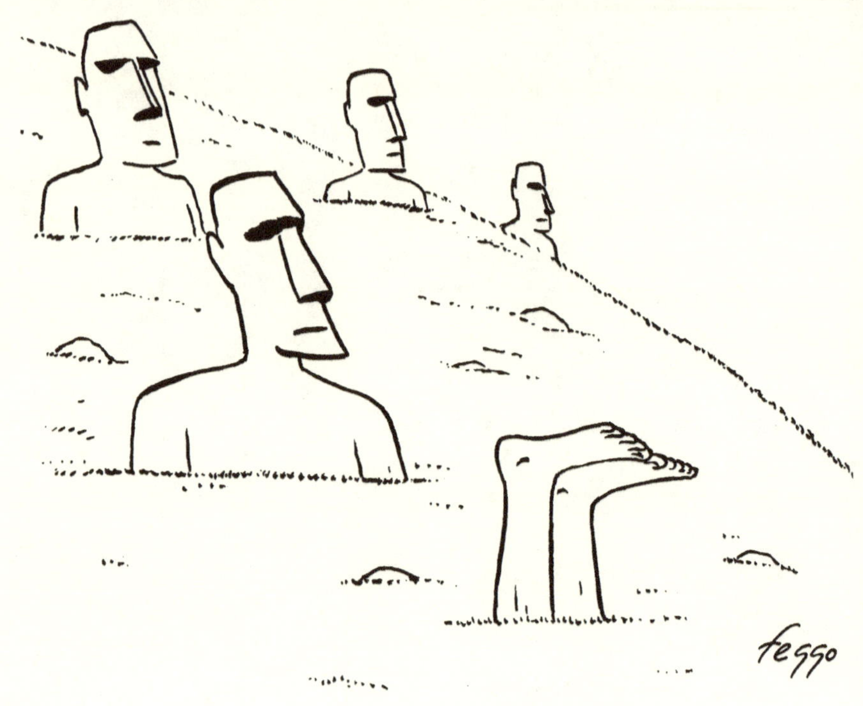
feggo

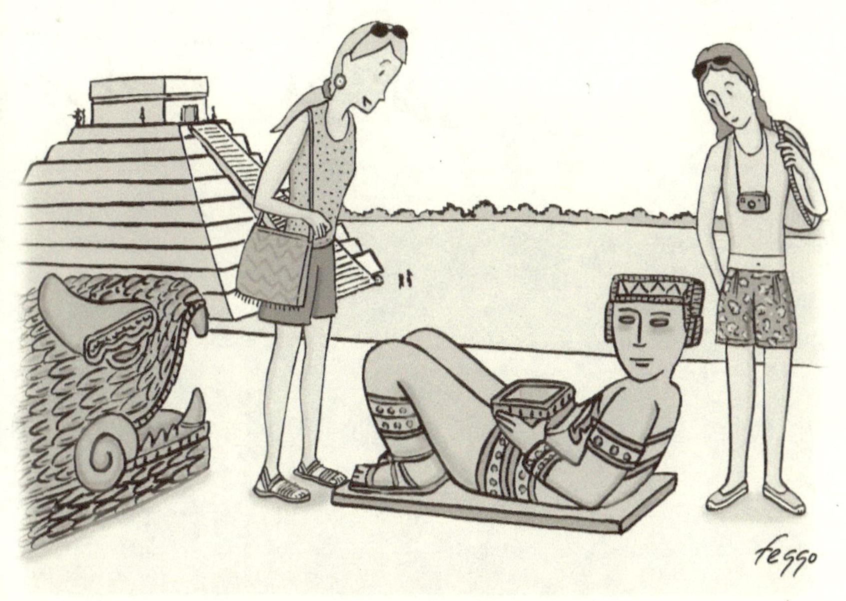

"Look, the Maya did Pilates!"

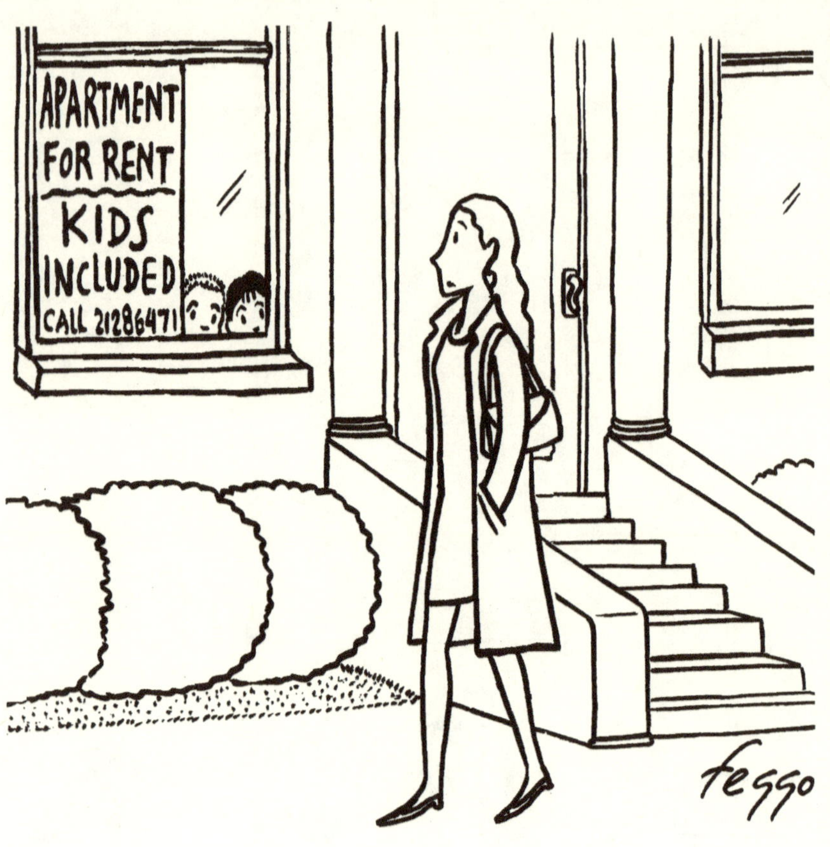
APARTMENT
FOR RENT
KIDS
INCLUDED
CALL 21286471
feggo

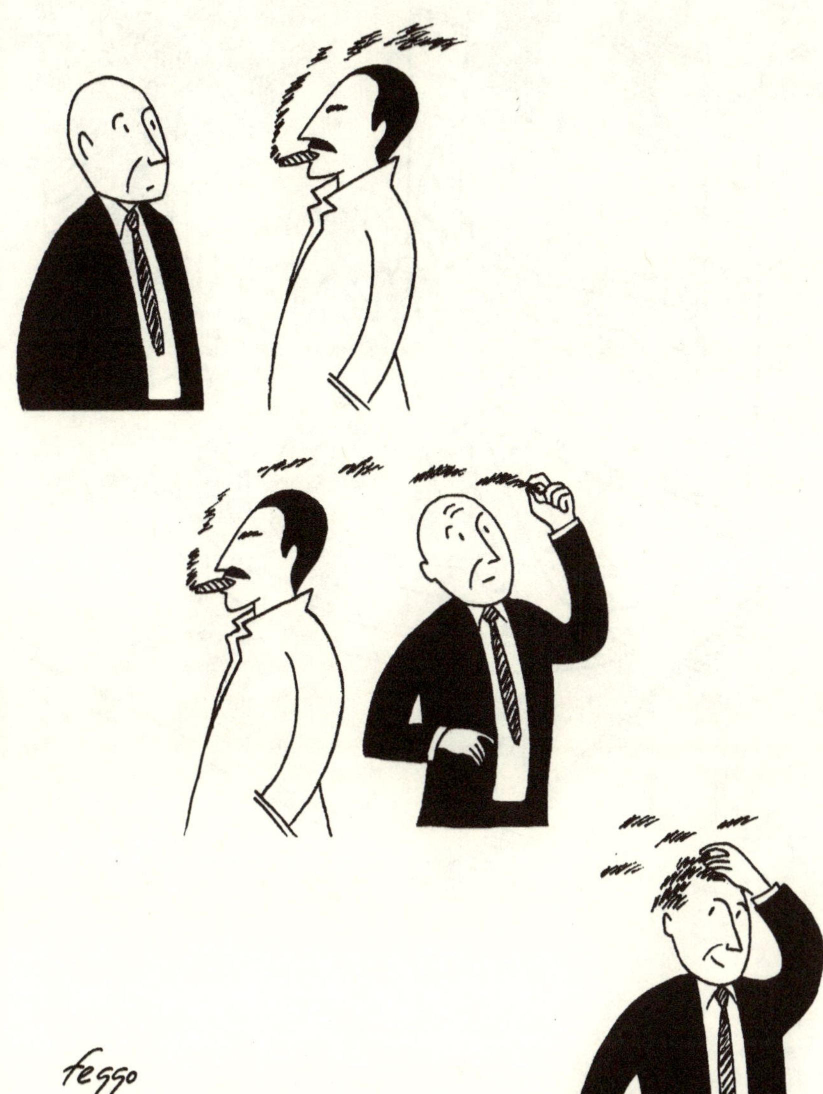
feggo

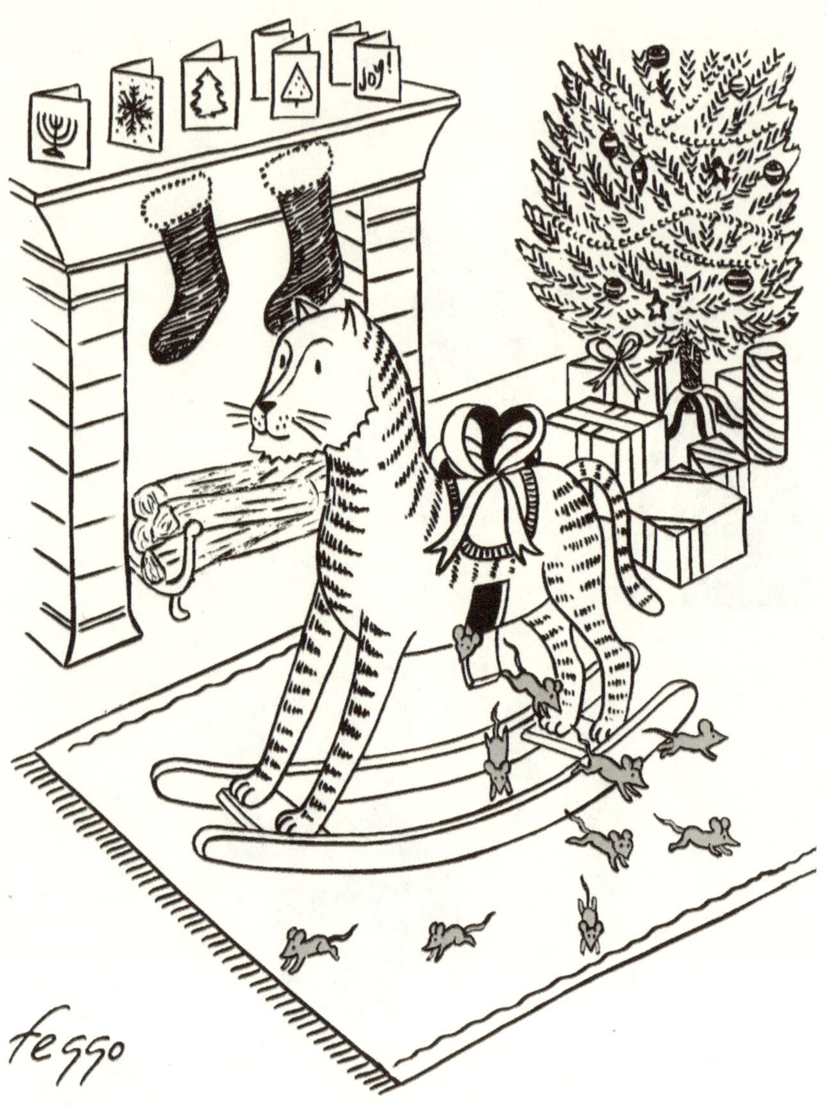
JOY!
feggo

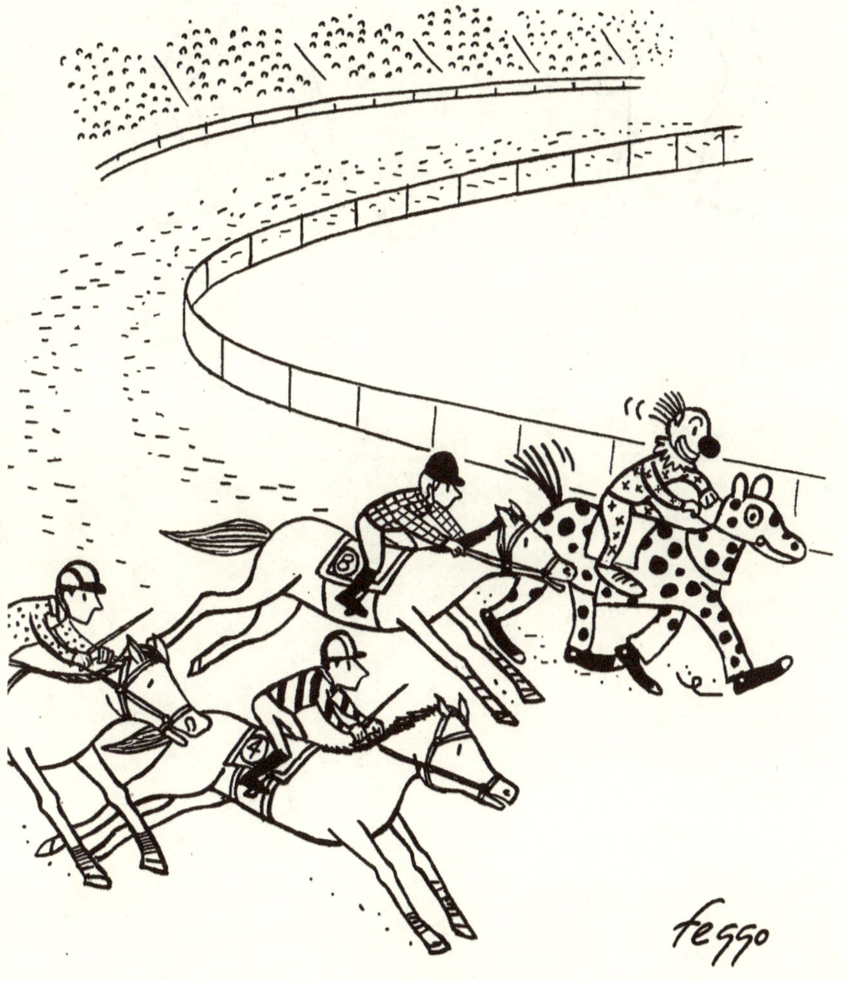
feggo

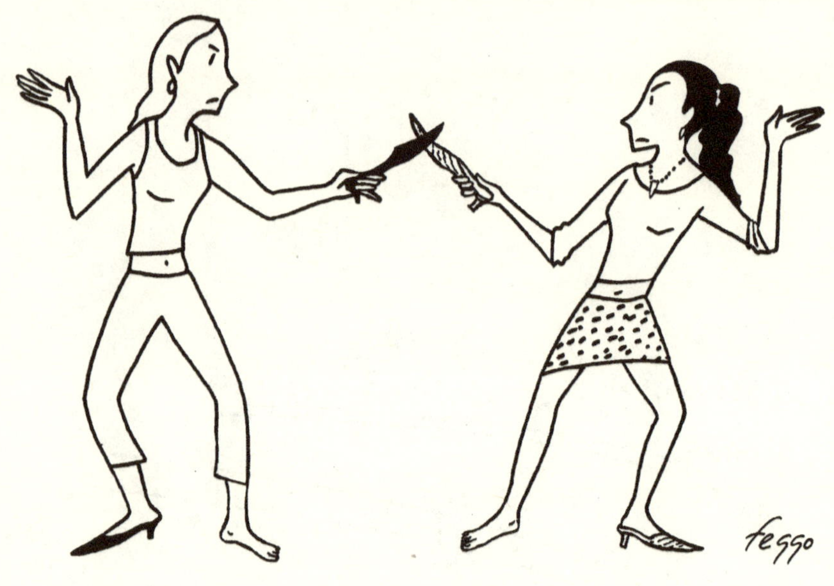
feggo

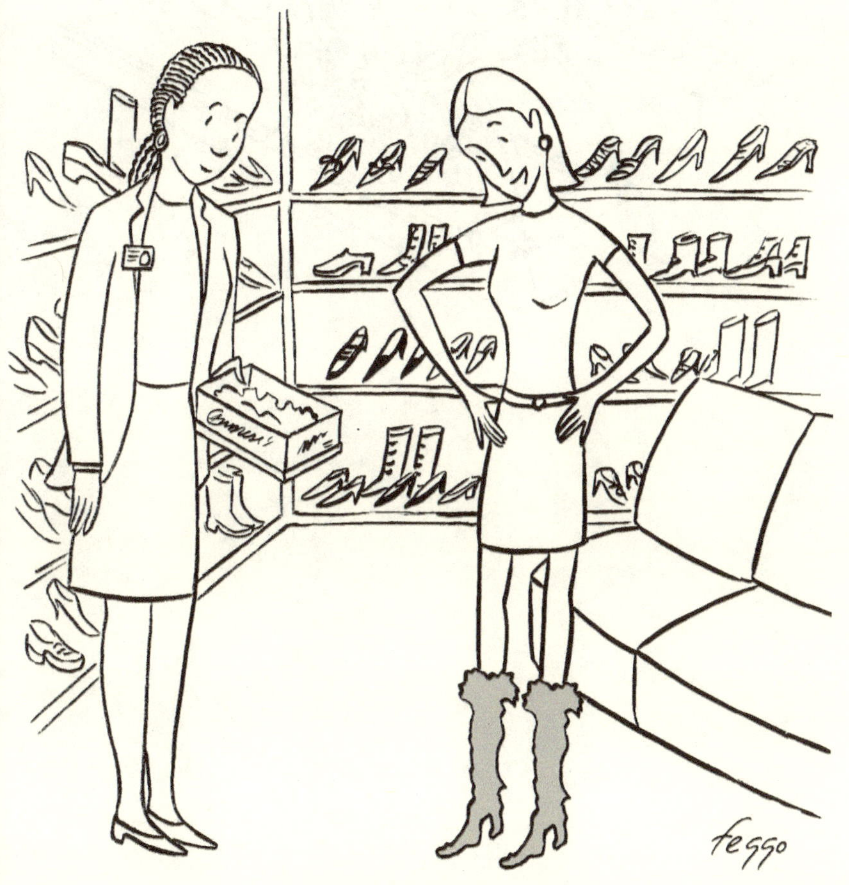

"I love Italian boots."

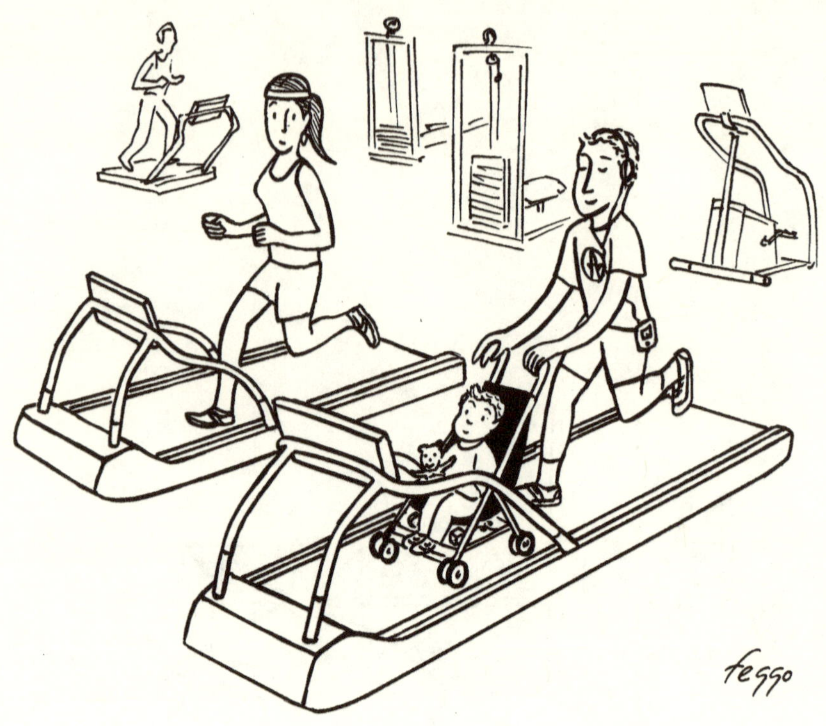
feggo

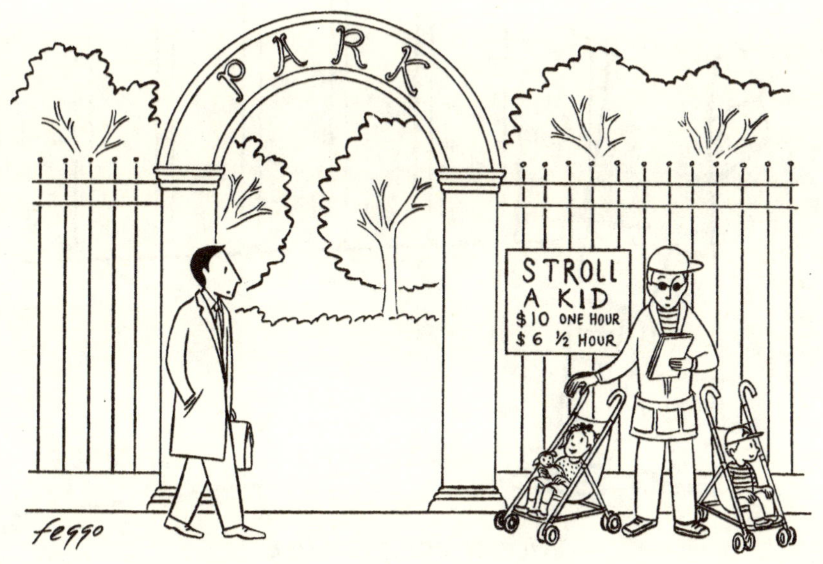
PARK
STROLL
A KID
$10 ONE HOUR
$6 ½ HOUR
feggo

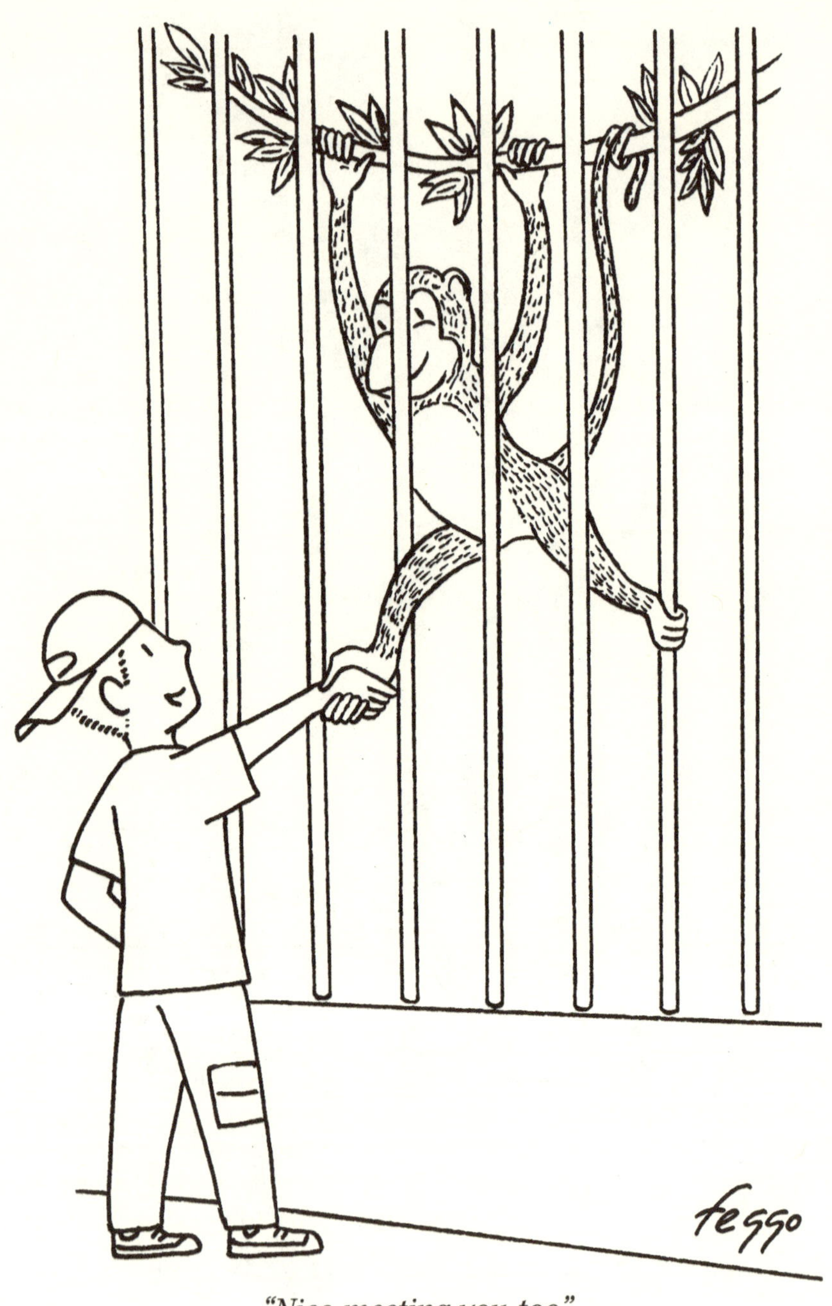

"Nice meeting you too."

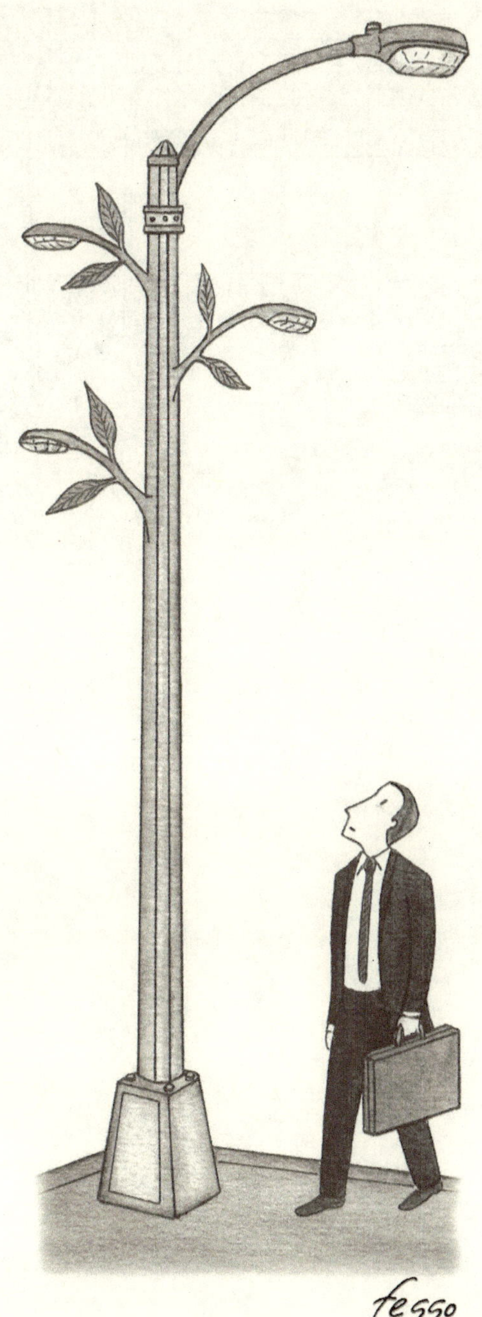

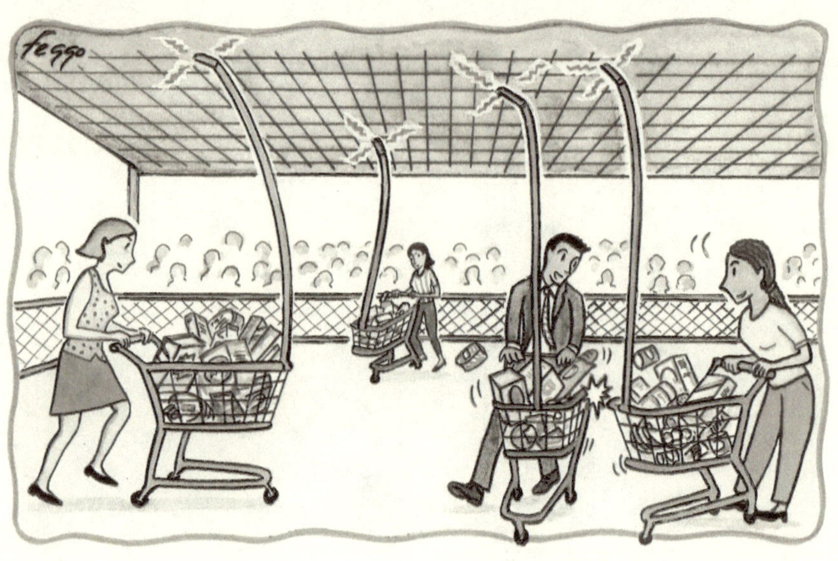
feggo

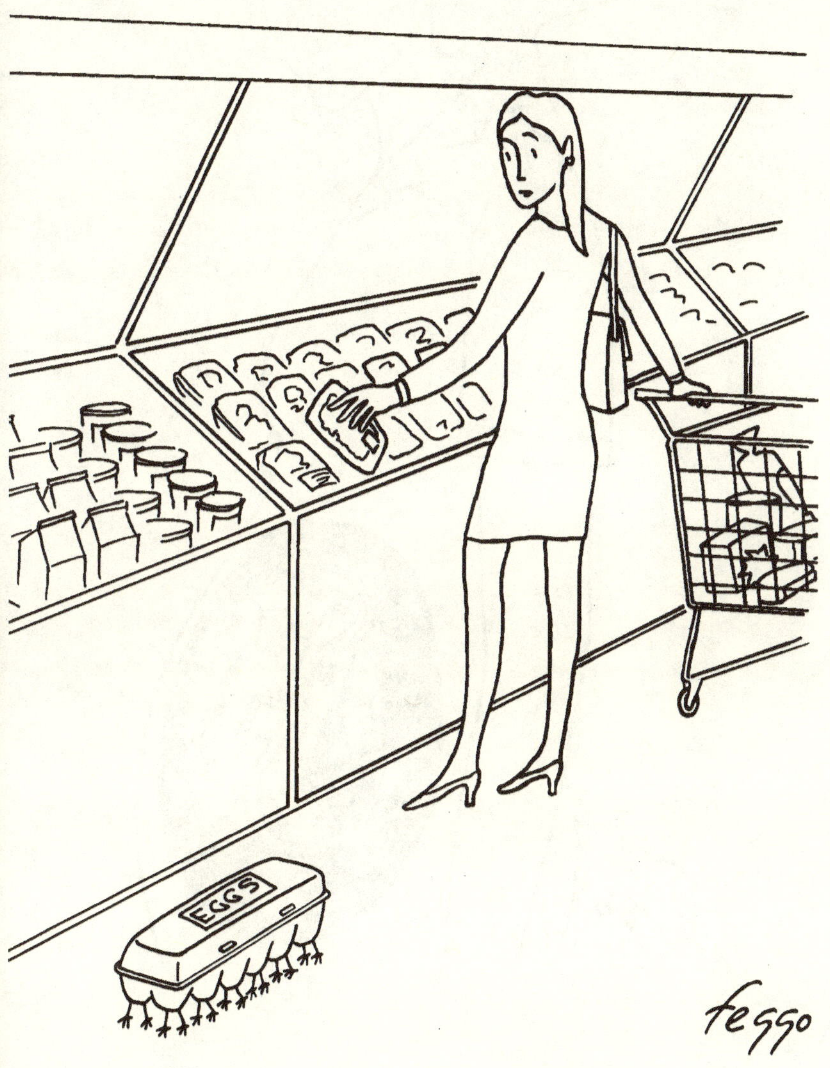
EGGS
feggo

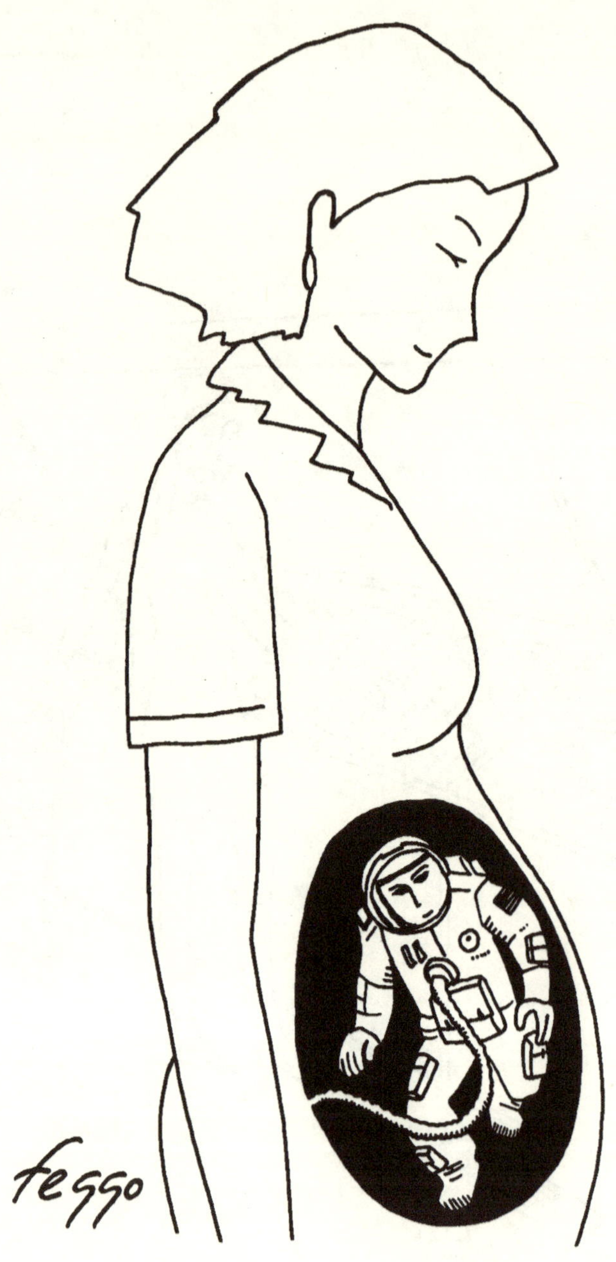
feggo

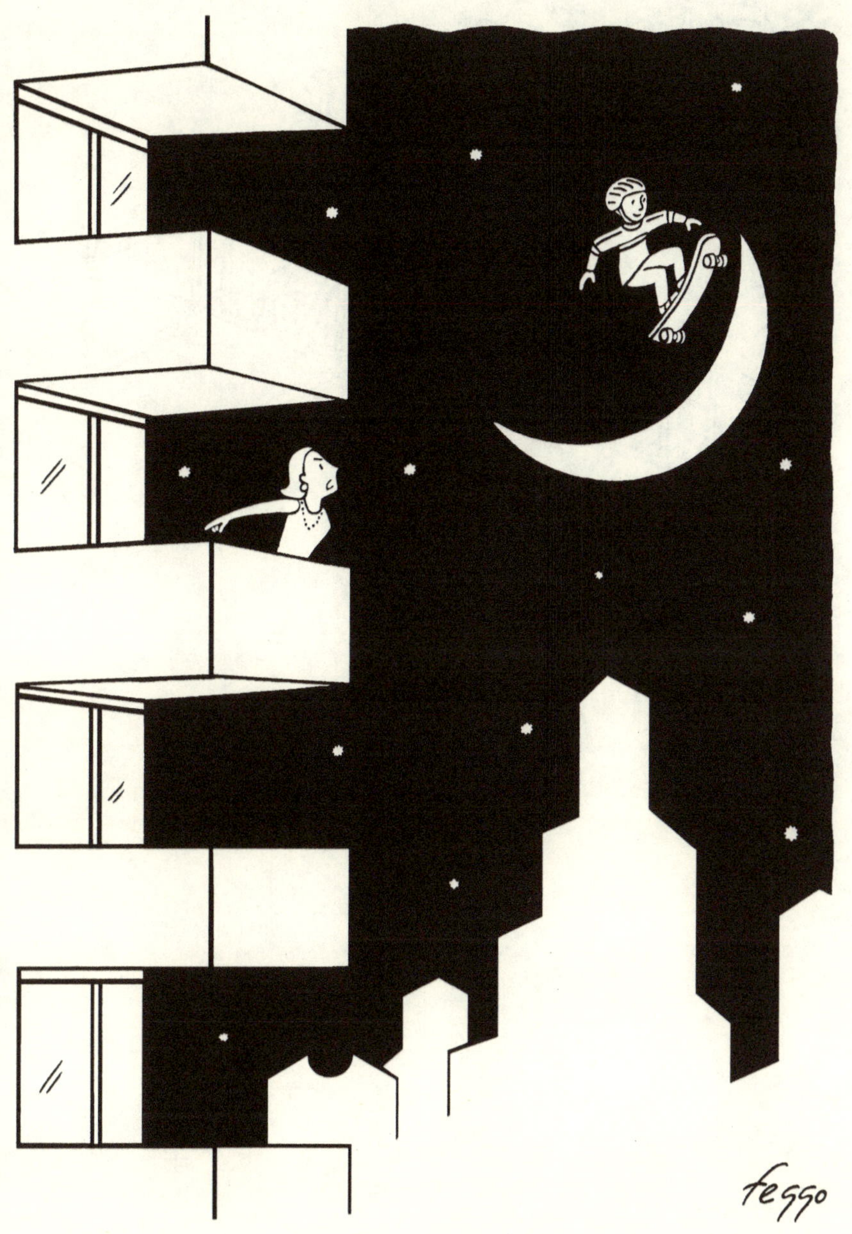
feggo

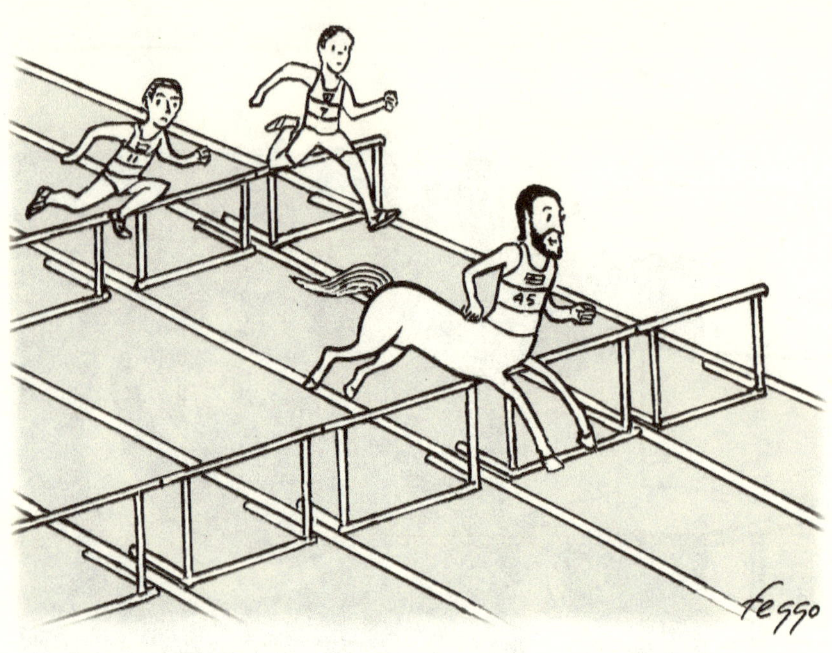
45
feggo

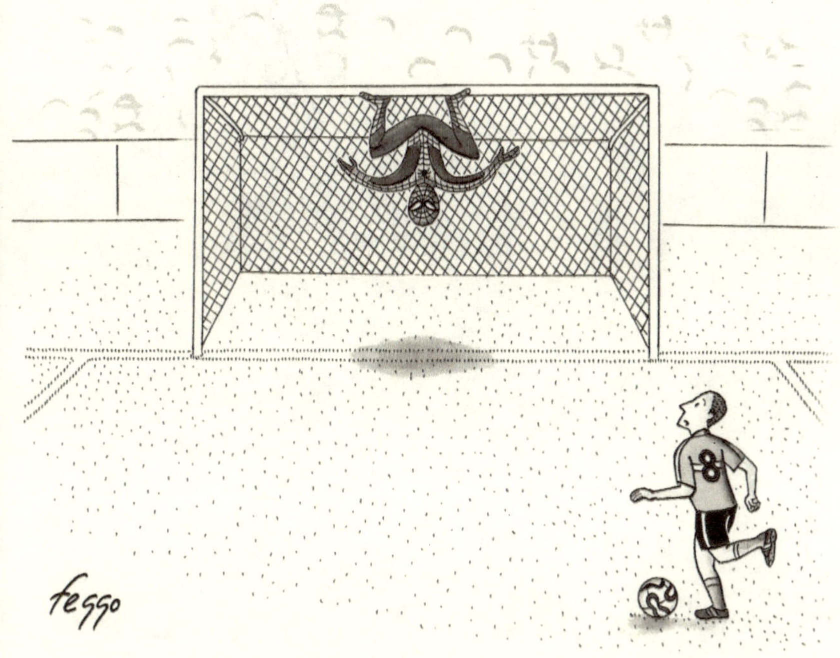
feggo

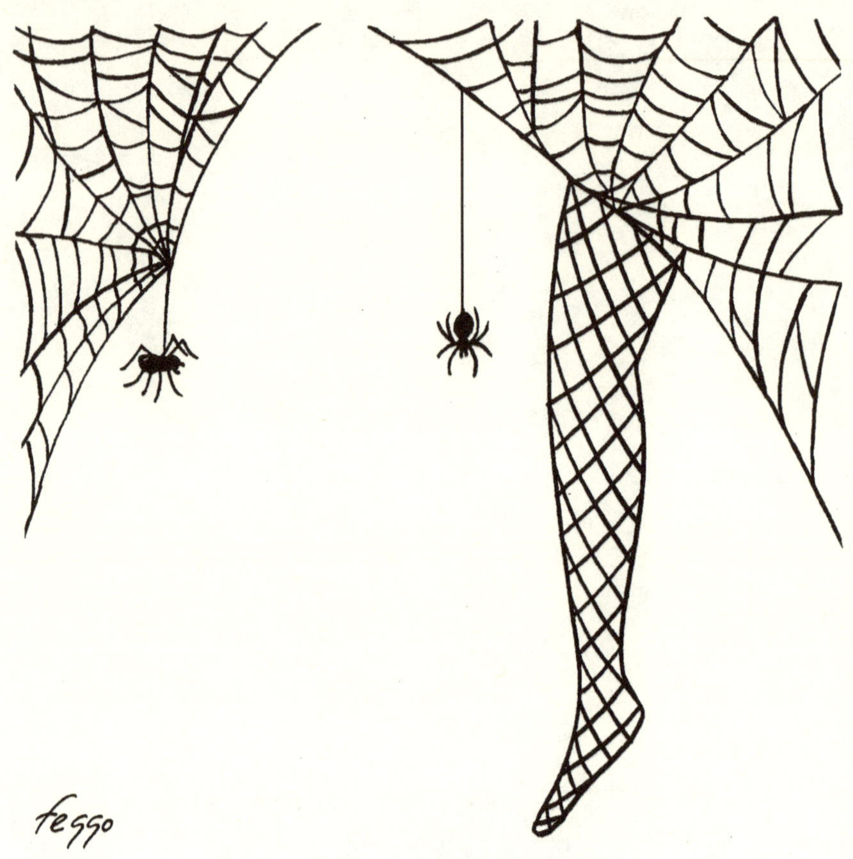
feggo

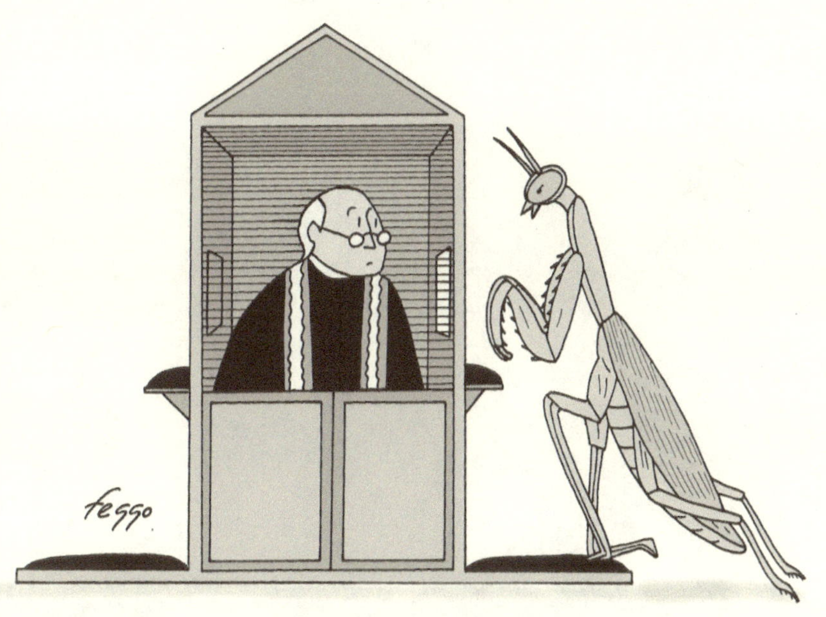

"I ate my husband."

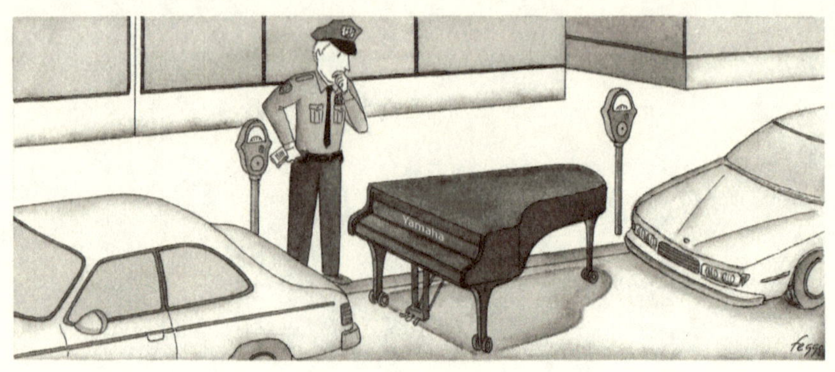
Yamaha

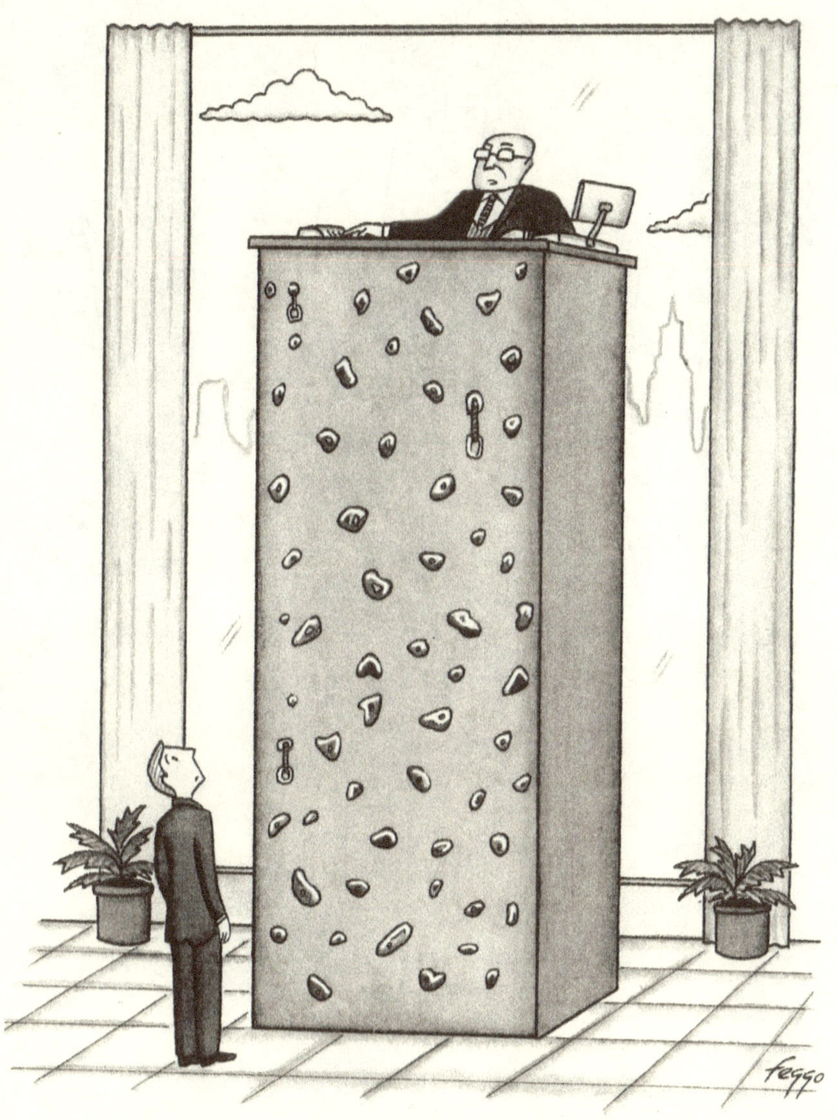

"Ascend, Collins."

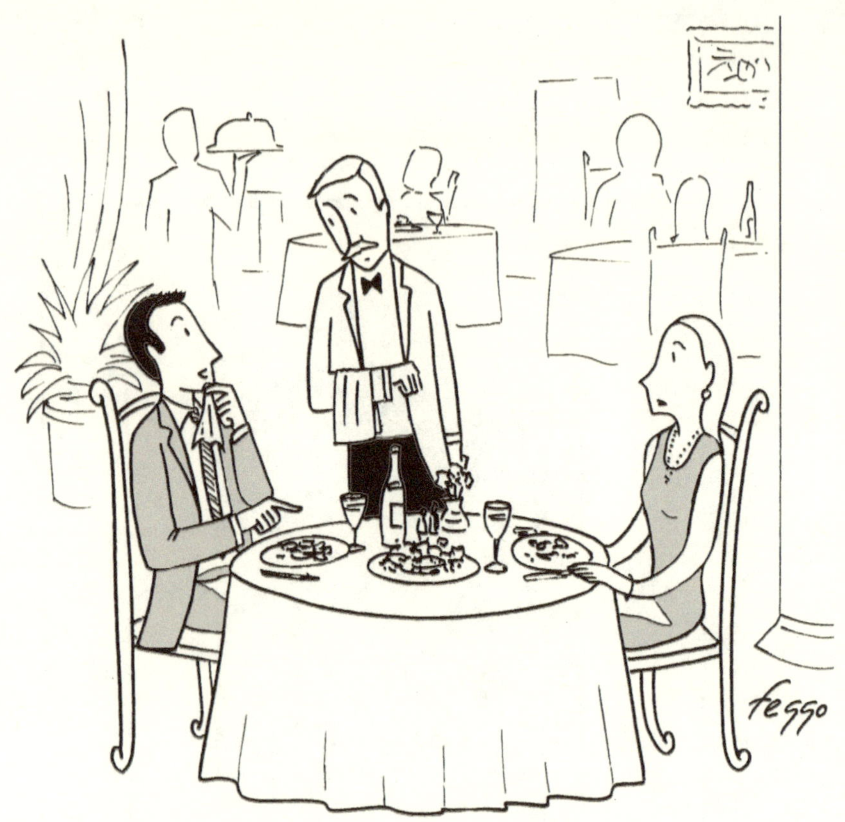

"Could you gift wrap these leftovers, please?"

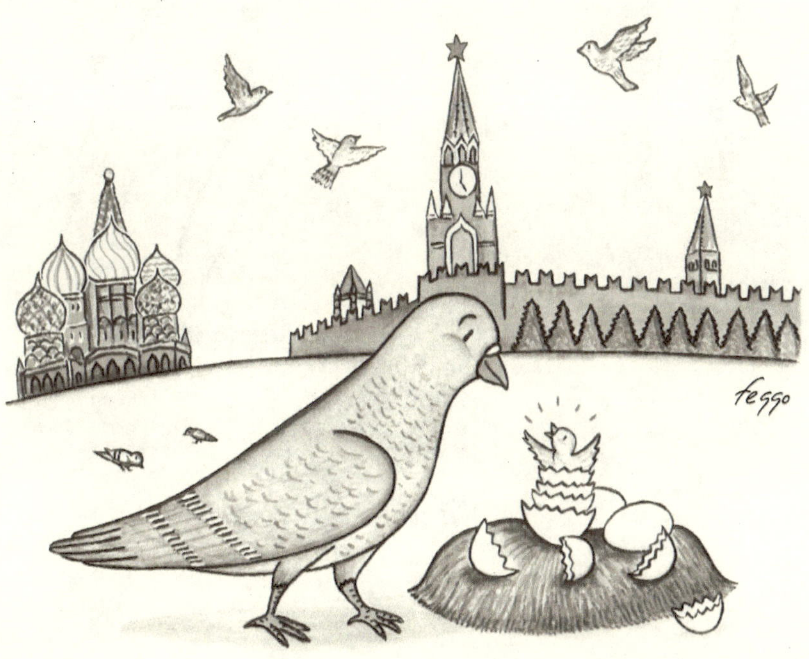
feggo

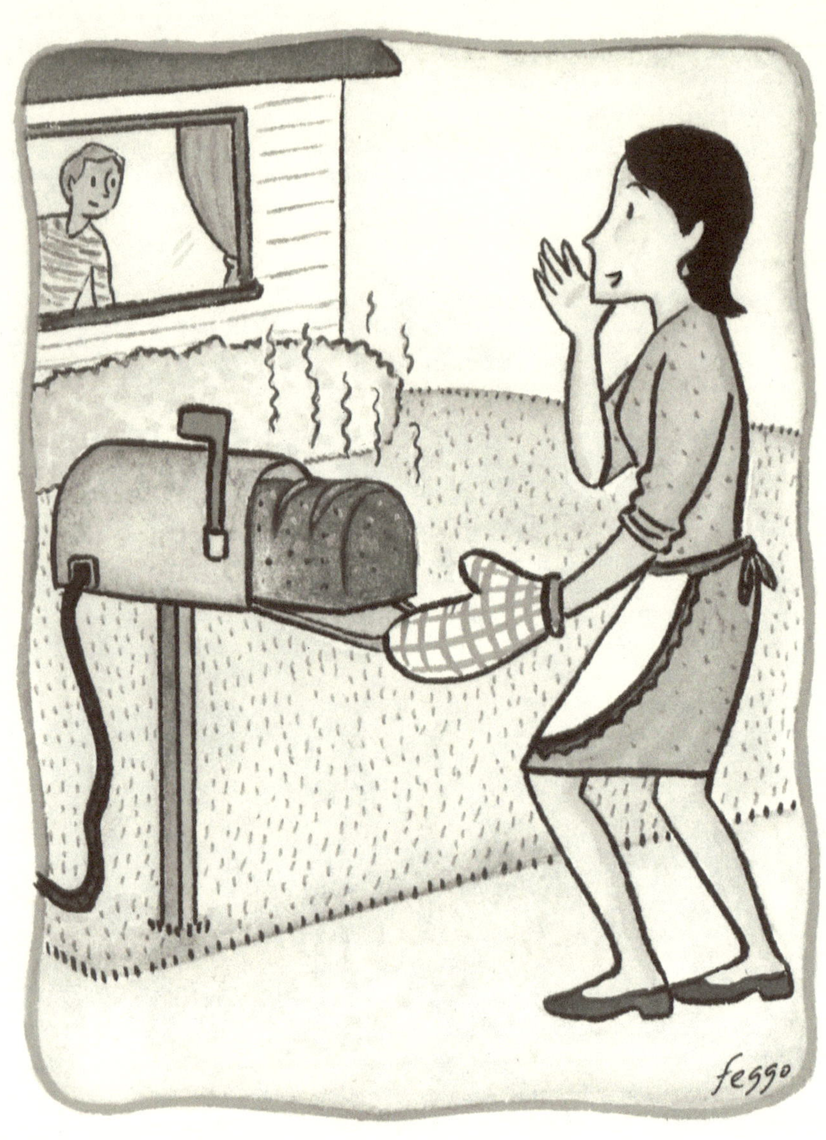

"It works!"

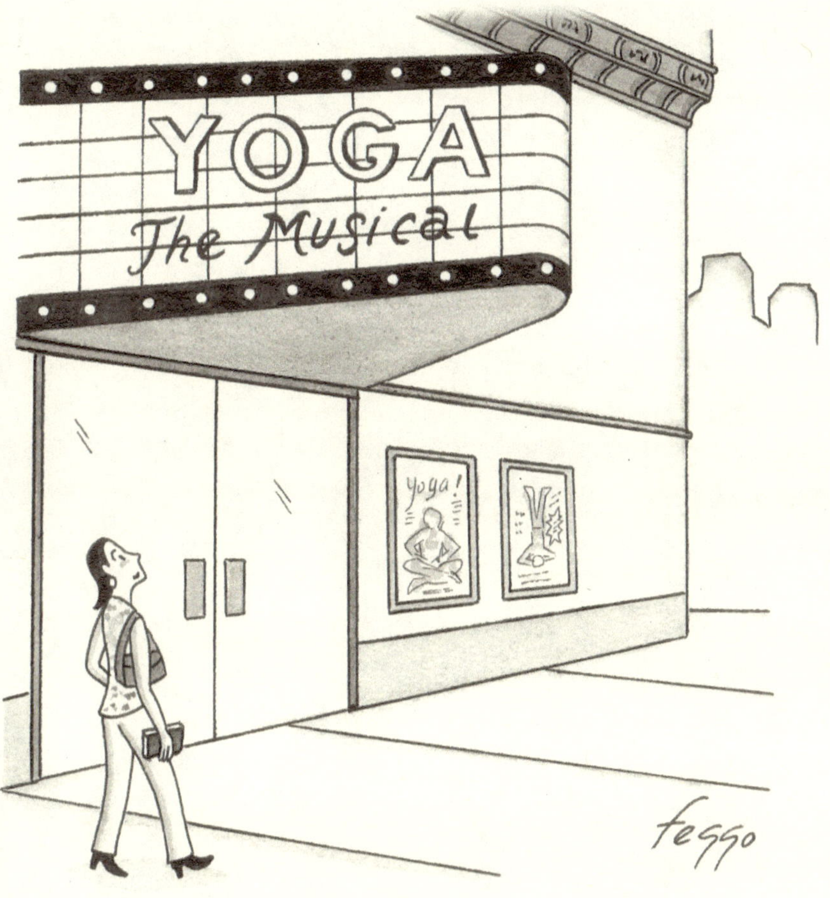
YOGA
The Musical
Yoga!
fesso

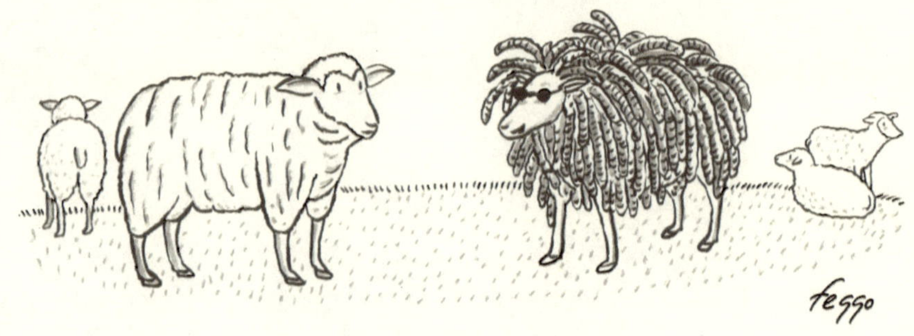

"Loved Jamaica!"

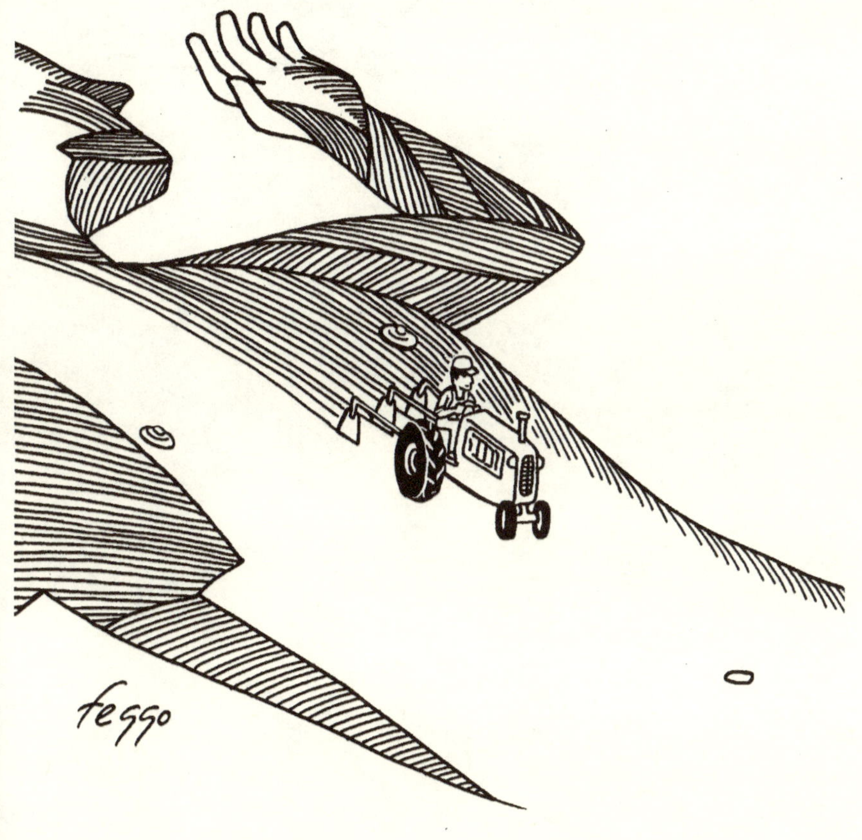
feggo

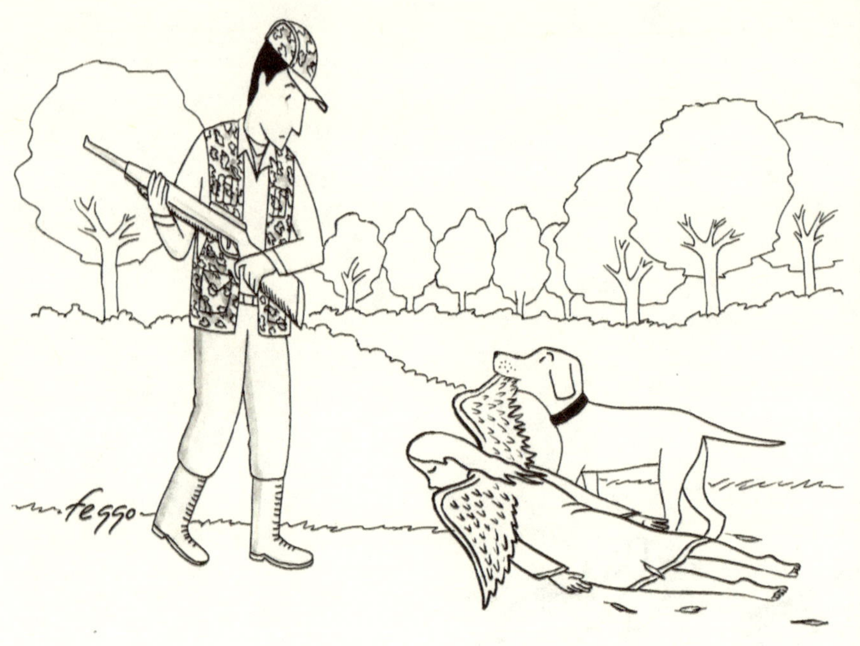
feggo

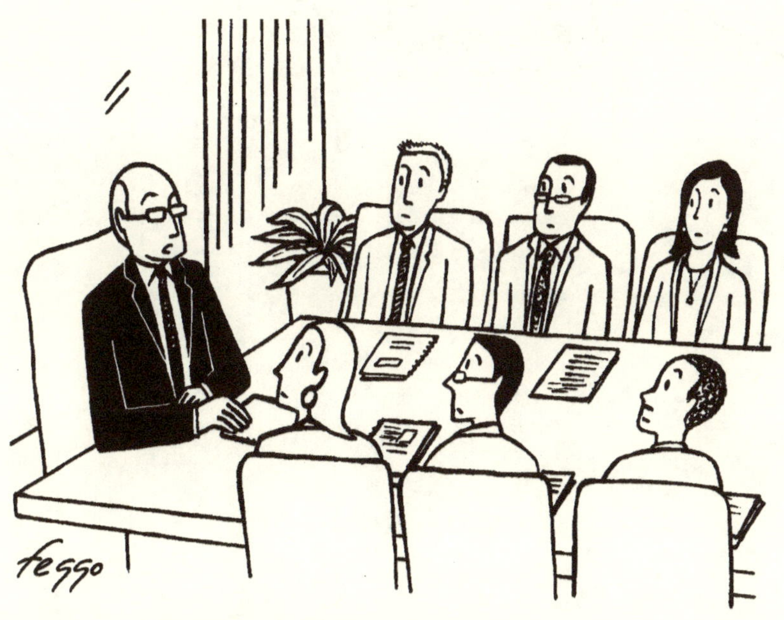

"Raise your hands those in favor of saving their soul rather than the company."

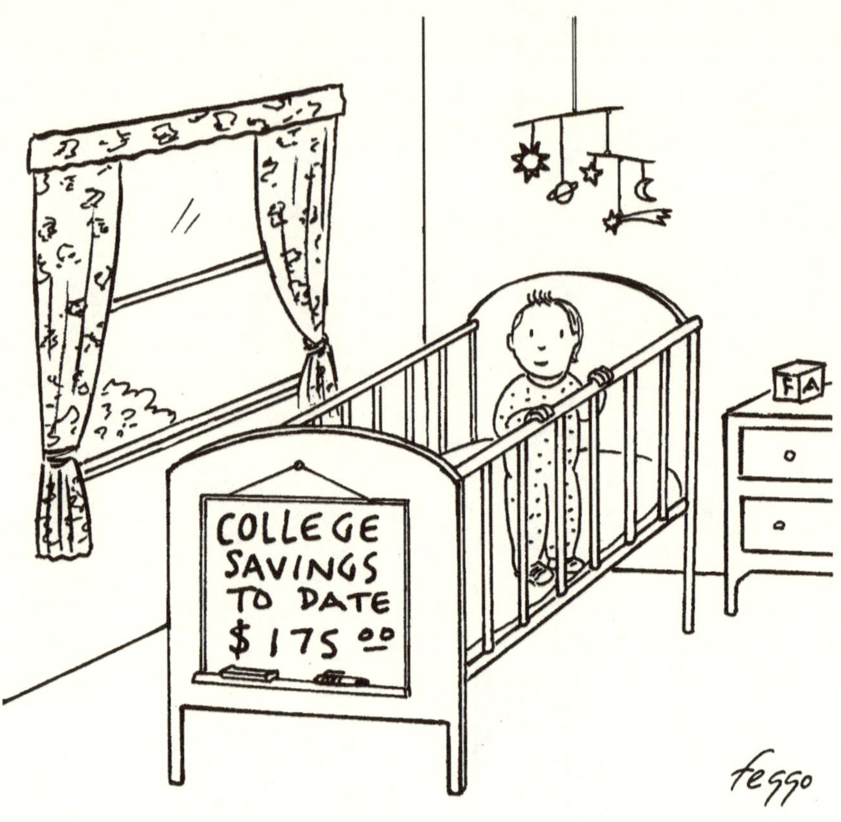
COLLEGE
SAVINGS
TO DATE
$175.00
FA
feggo

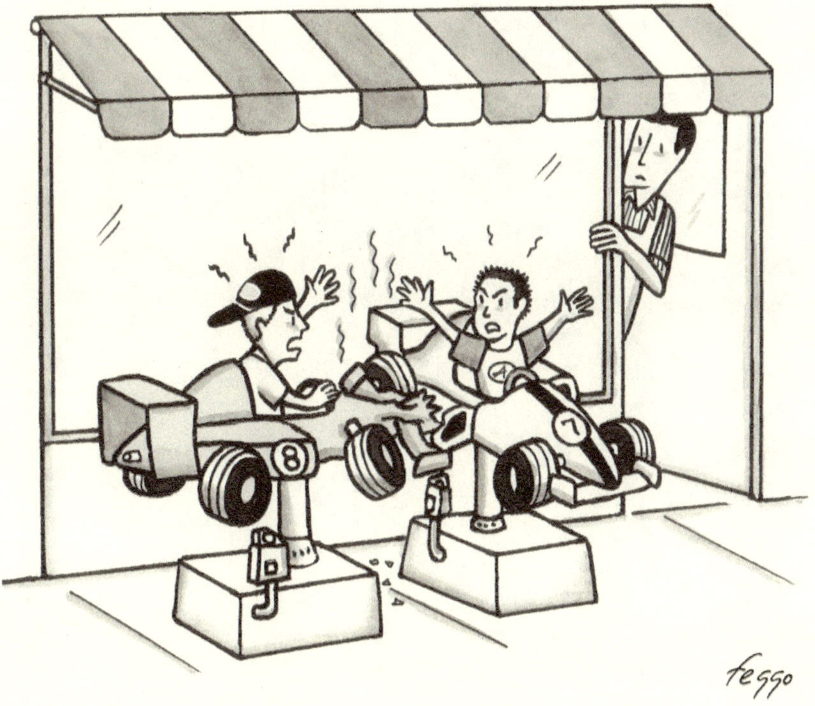
8
7
feggo

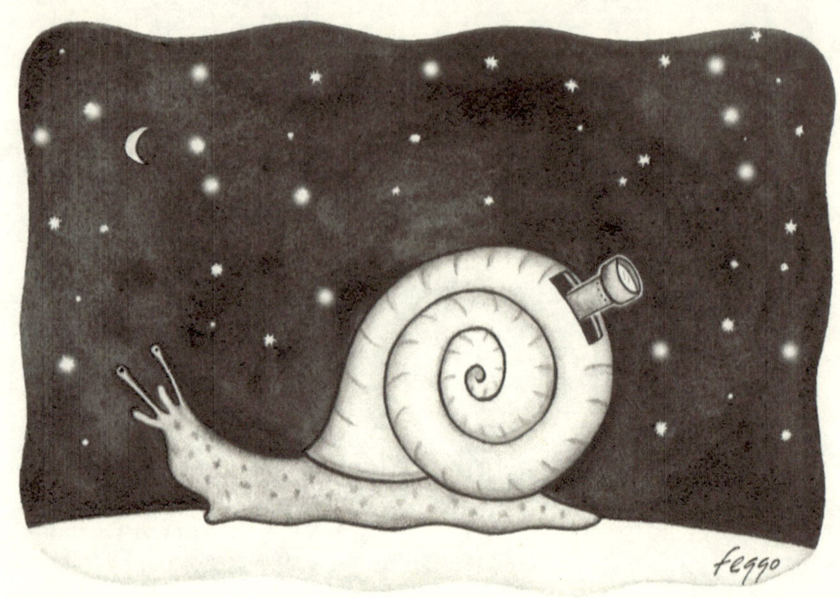
feggo

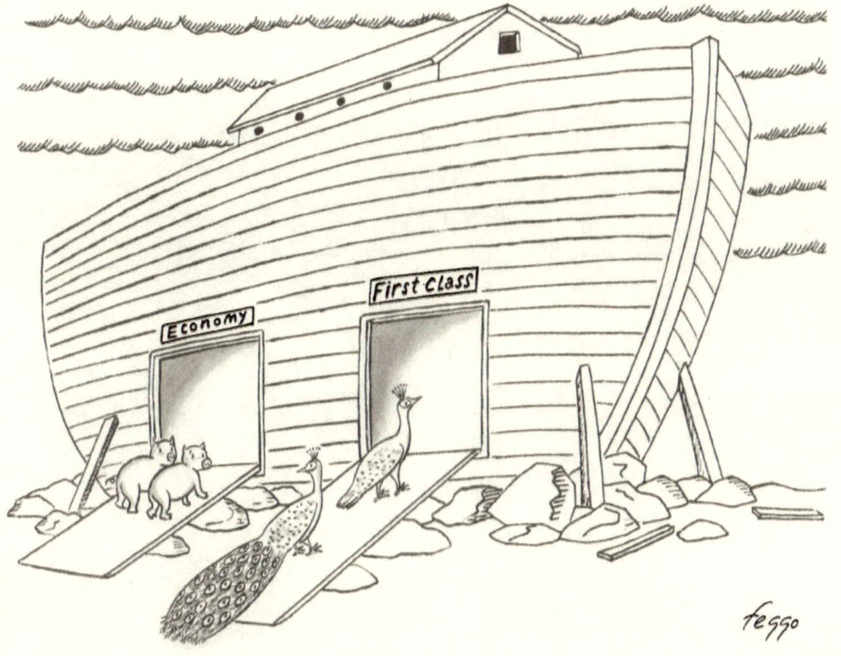
Economy
First Class
feggo

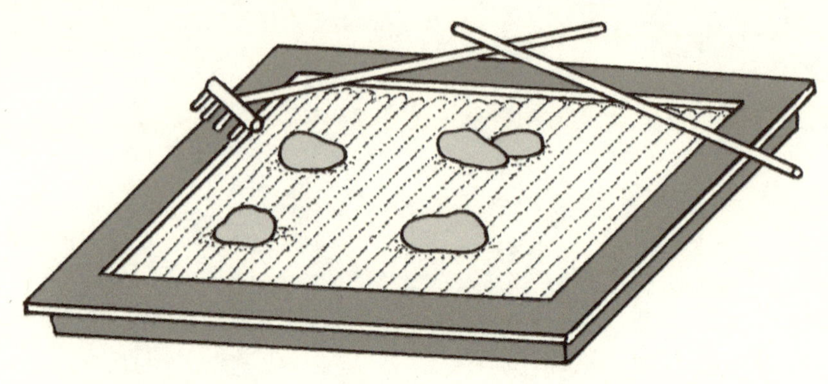

MINIATURE COCAINE ZEN GARDEN

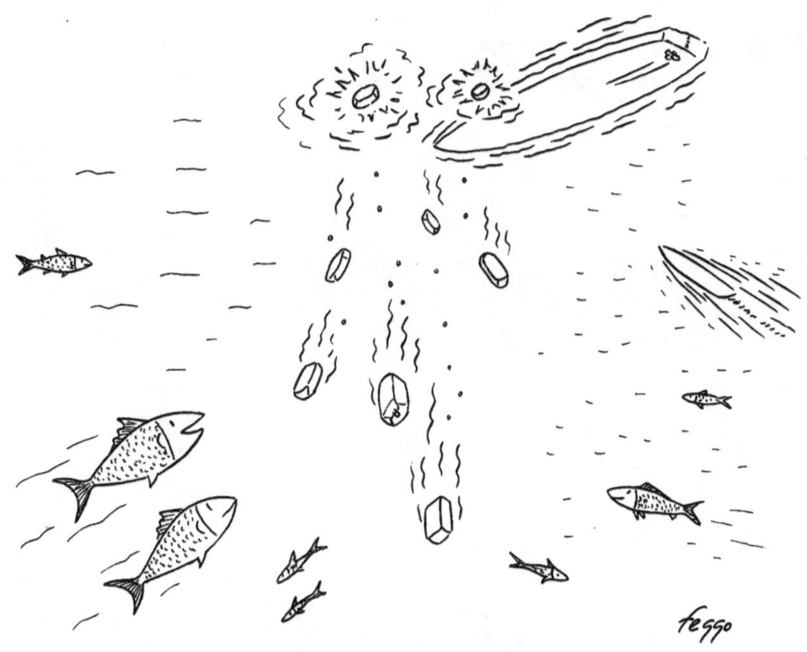

"Woha! Drugs overboard!"

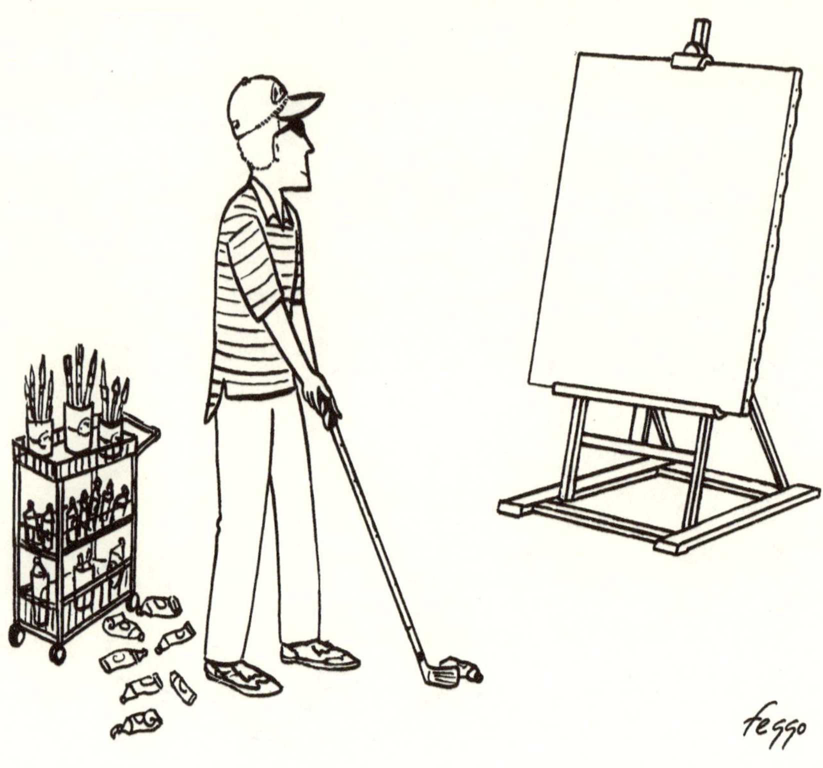
feggo

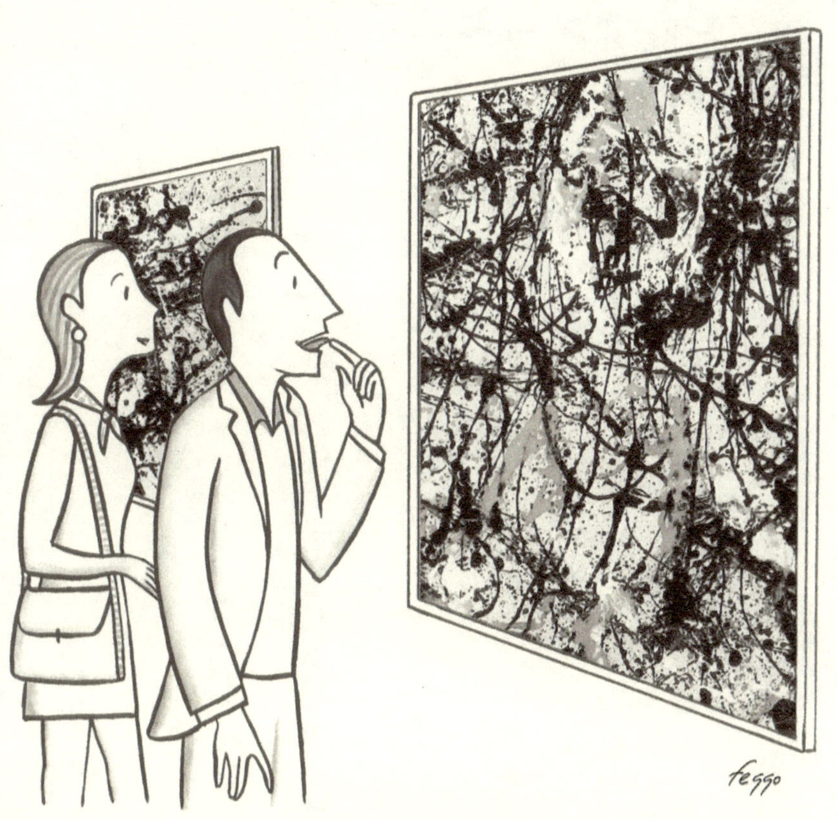

"It's Chicken Mole!"

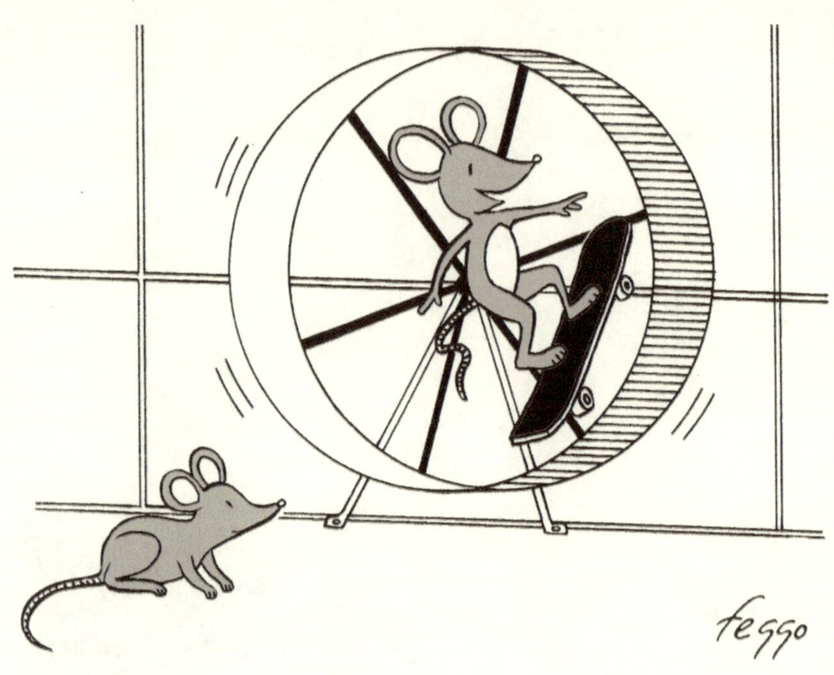
feggo

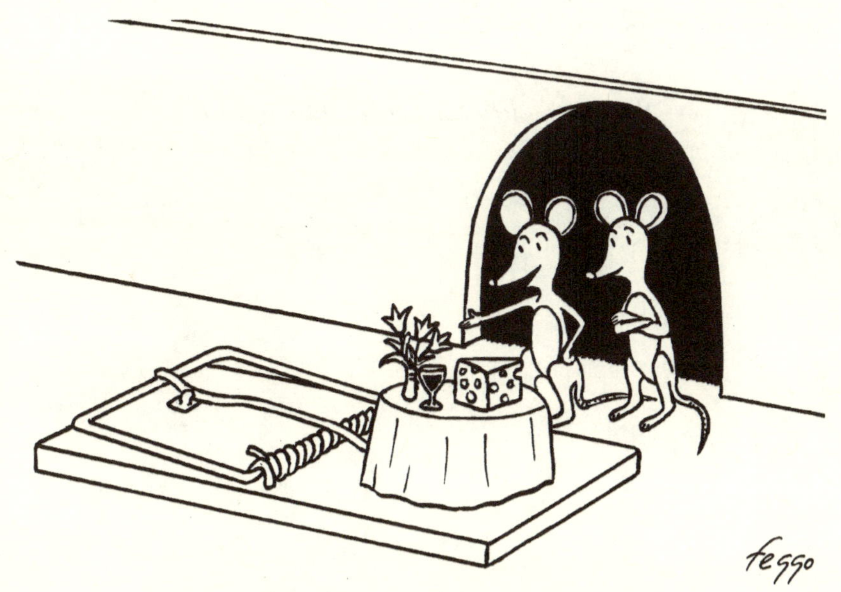

"Now, this is a trap worth dying for."

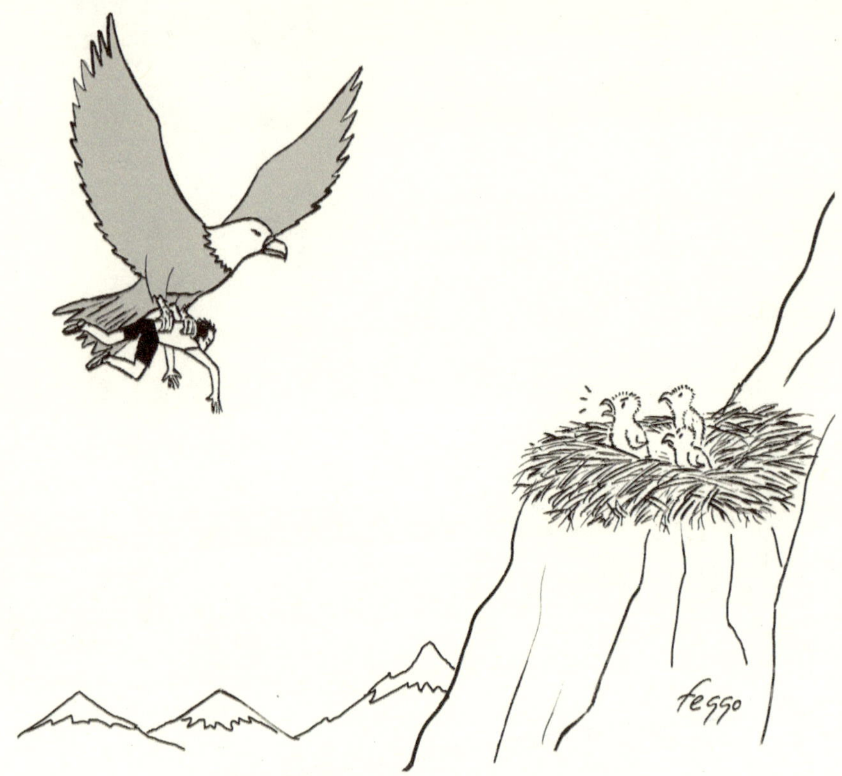

"Not rock climber for dinner again!"

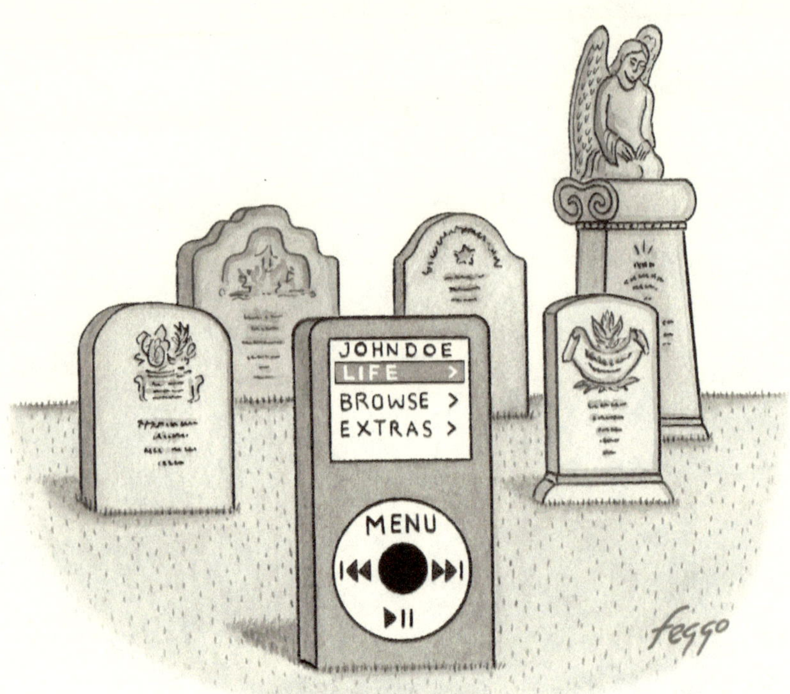
JOHNDOE
LIFE >
BROWSE >
EXTRAS >
MENU
feggo

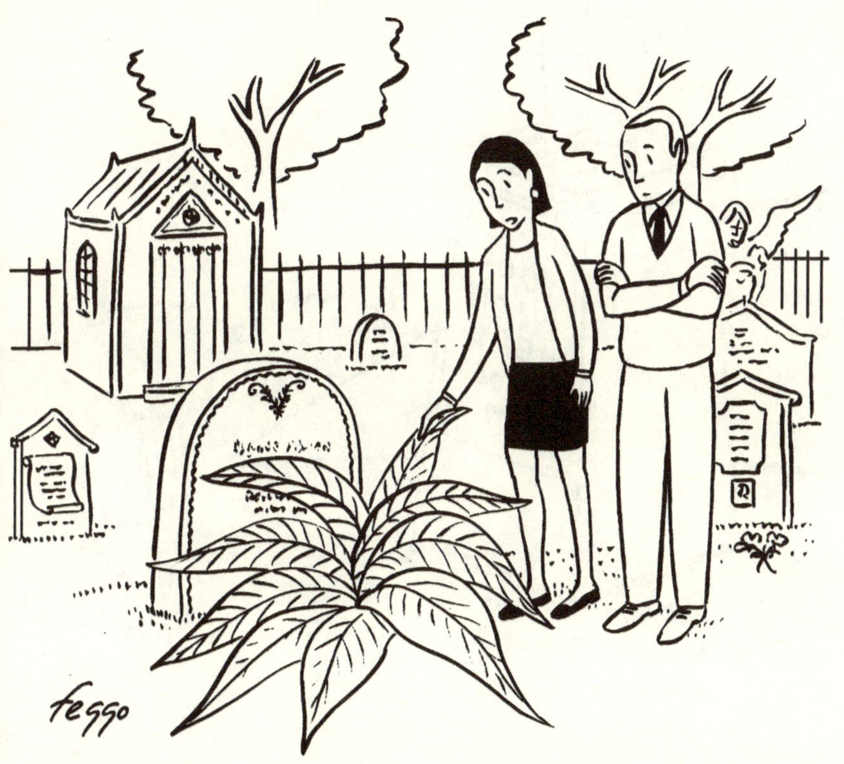

"It must be a tobacco plant, he was a heavy smoker."

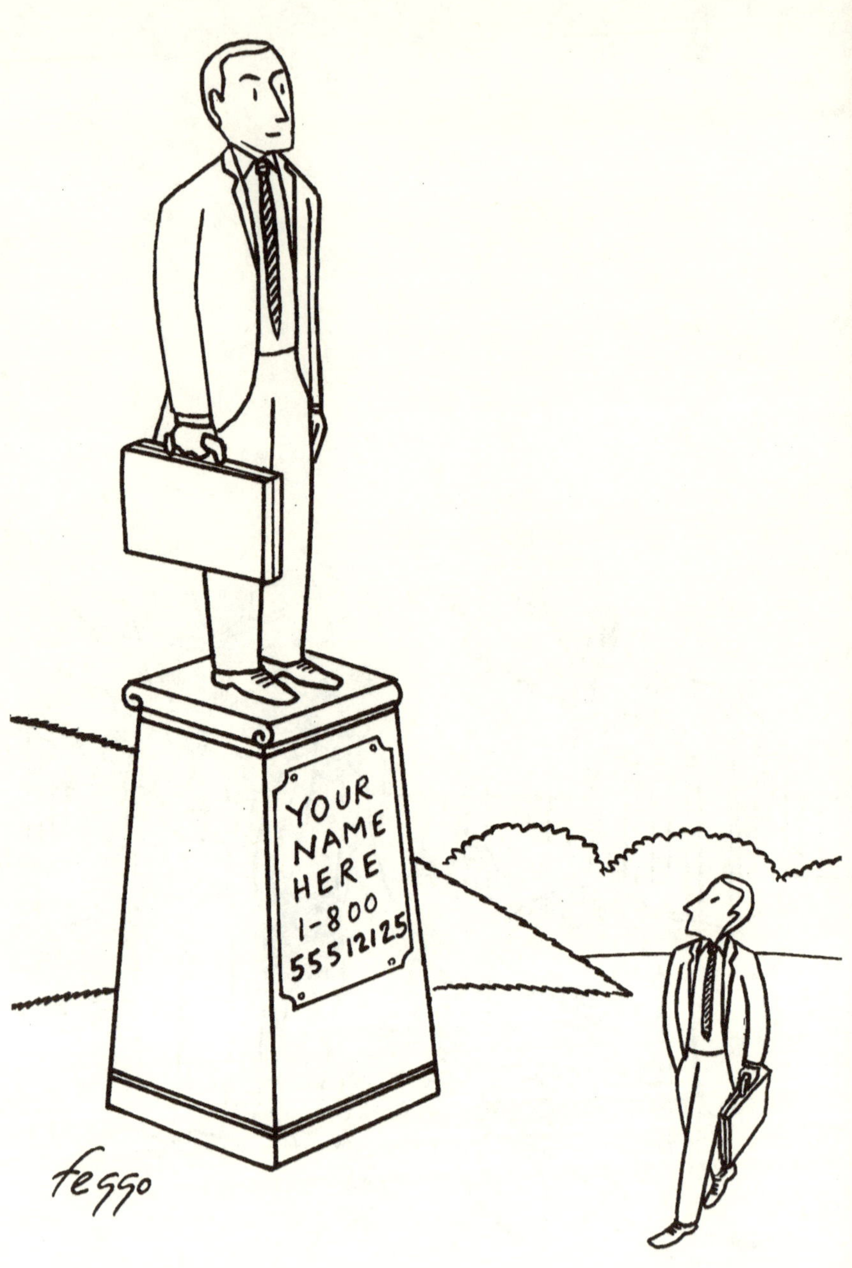
YOUR
NAME
HERE
1-800
55512125
feggo

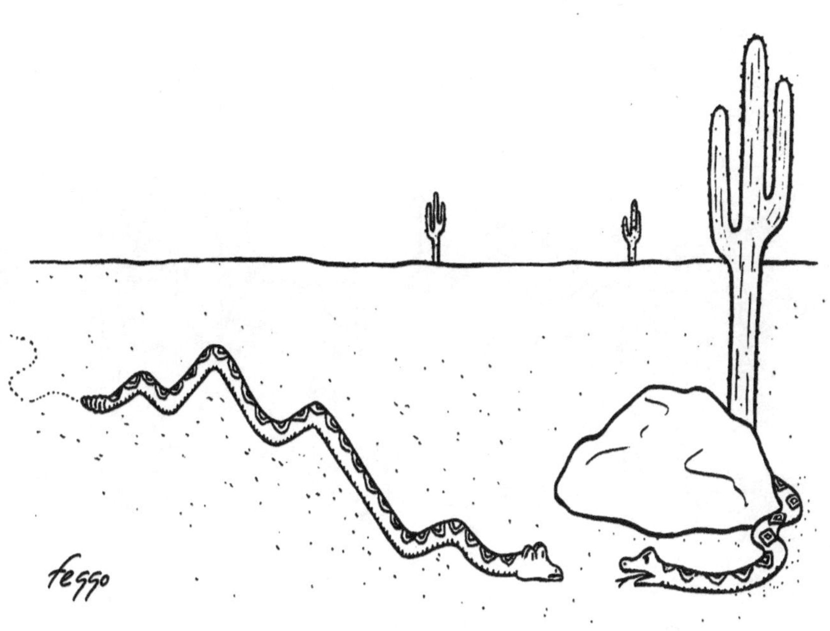

"Get your mind off the market!"

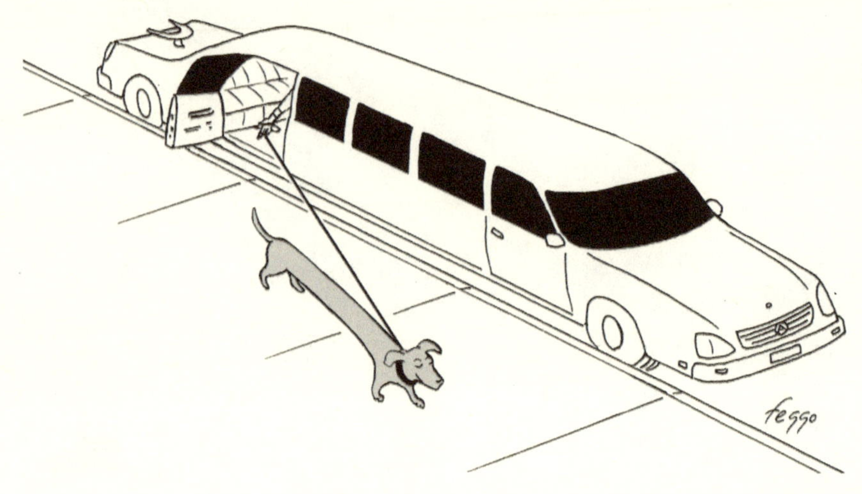
feggo

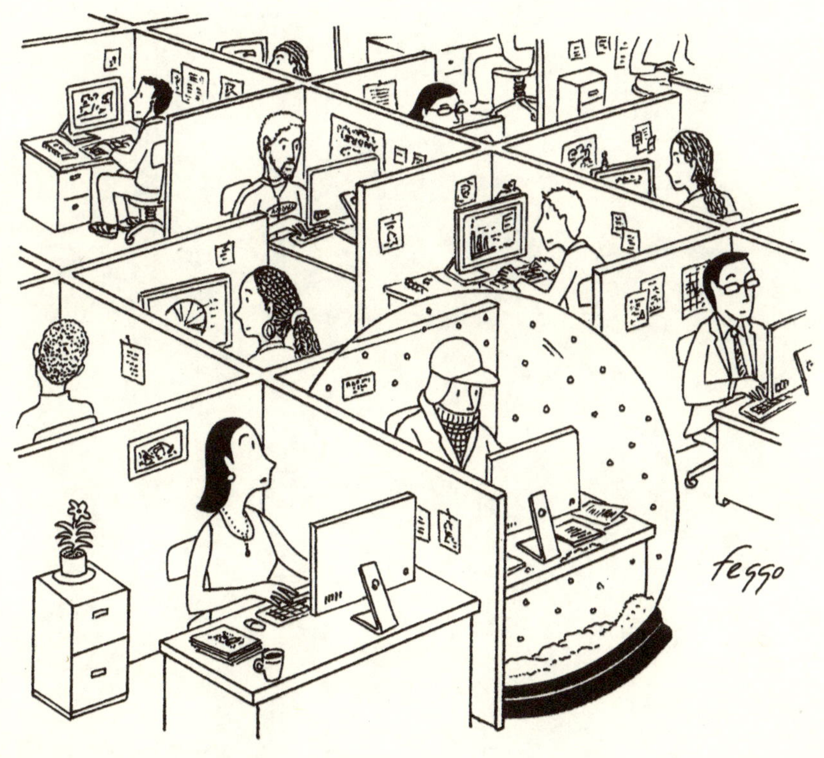
feggo

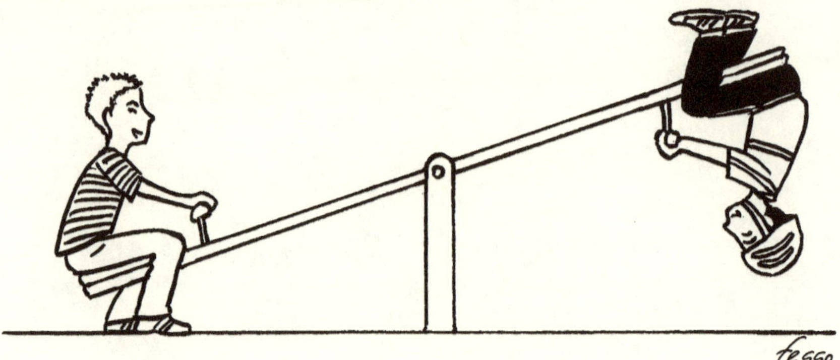

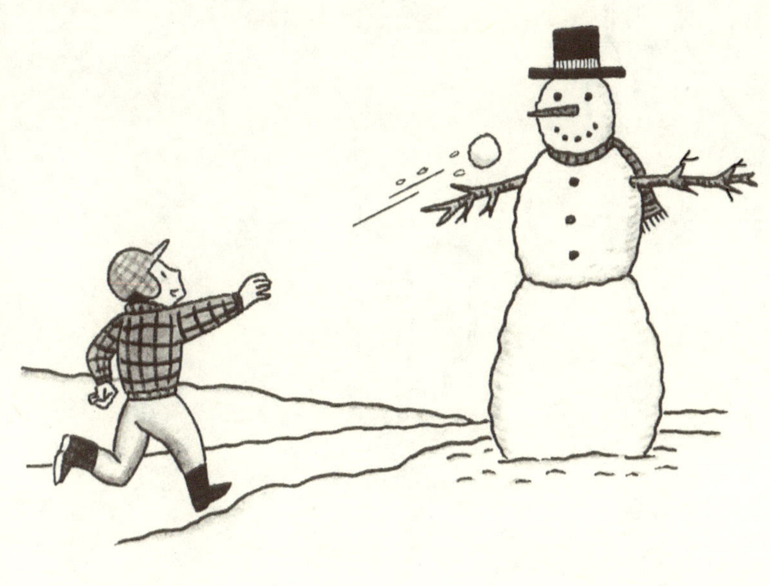

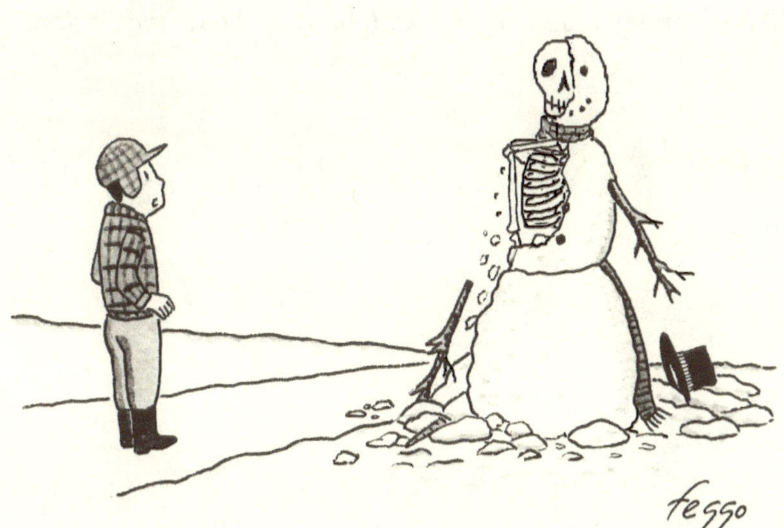
feggo

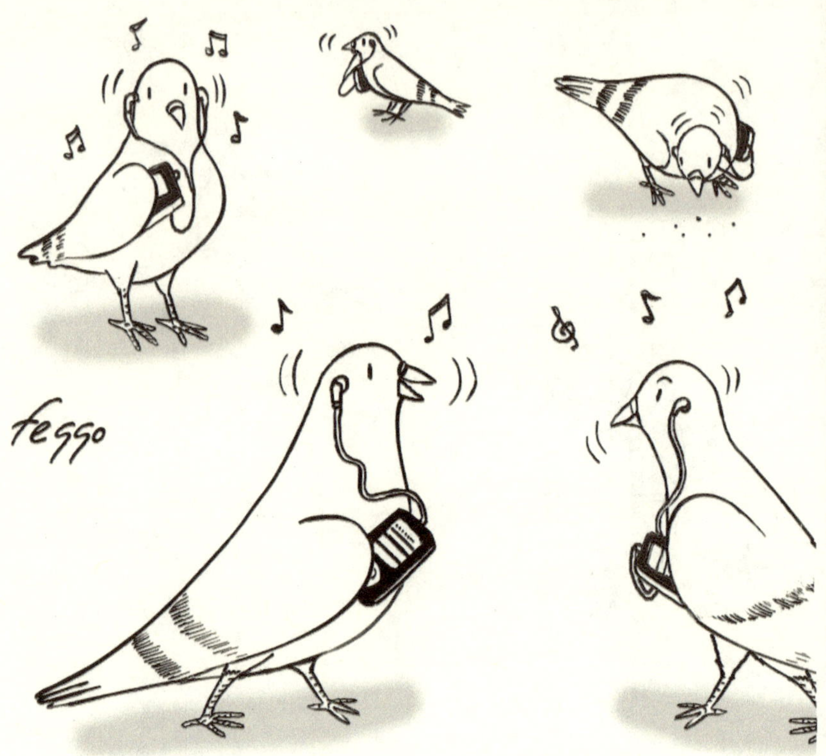

"What's on my iPod? The Byrds, Counting Crows, the Eagles . . ."

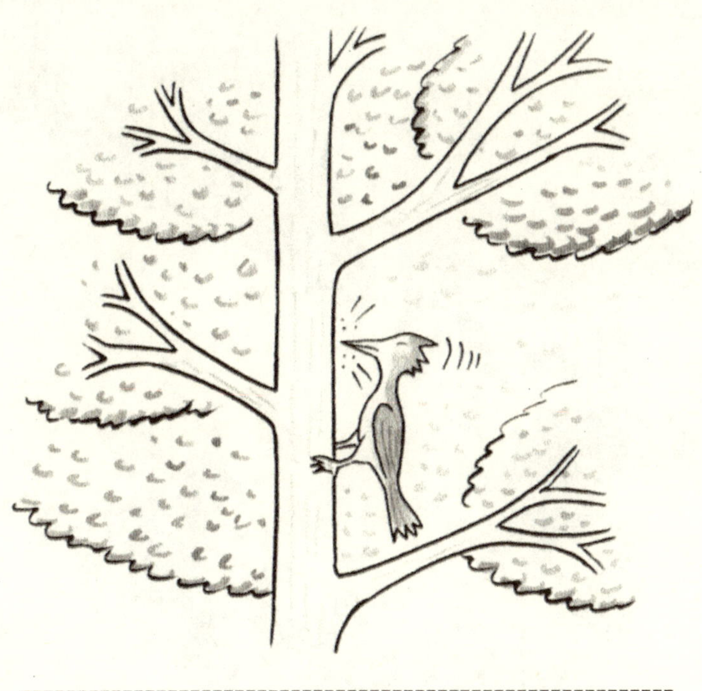

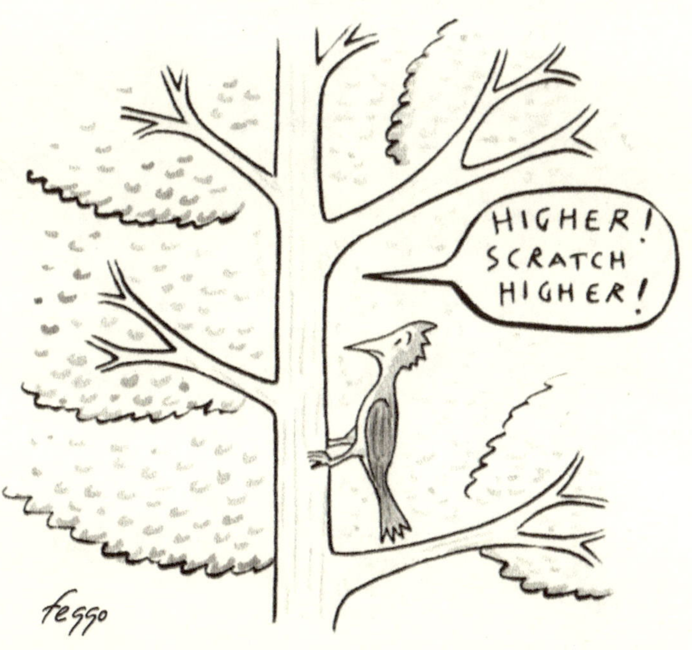
HIGHER! SCRATCH HIGHER!
feggo

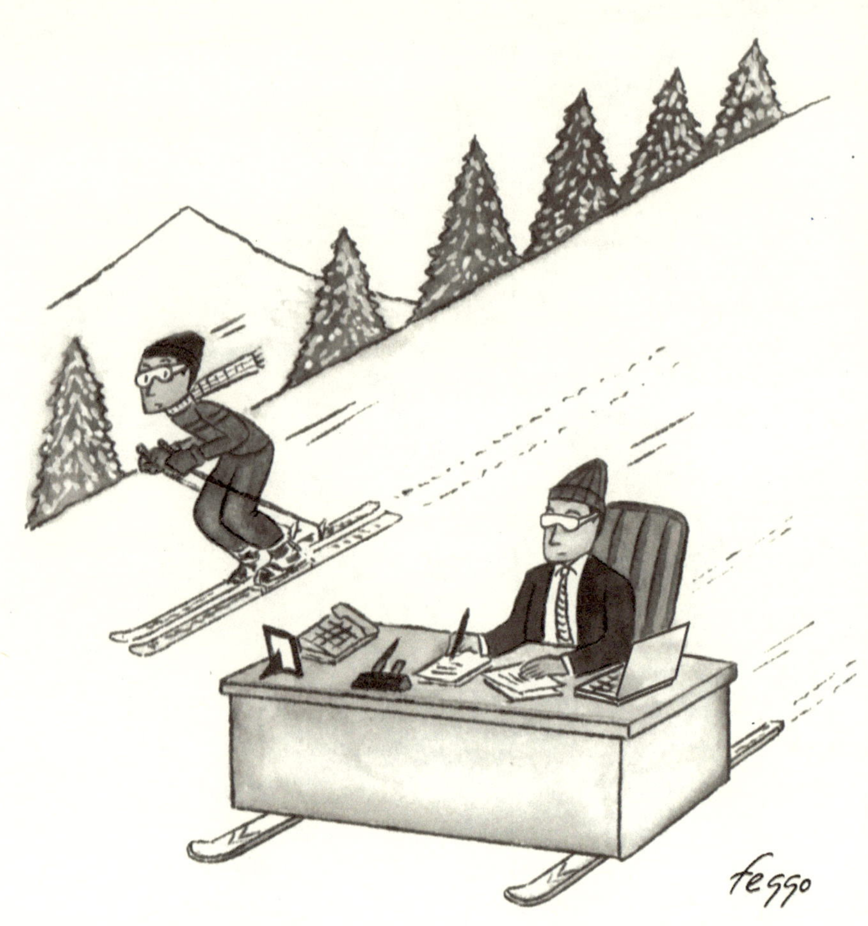
feggo

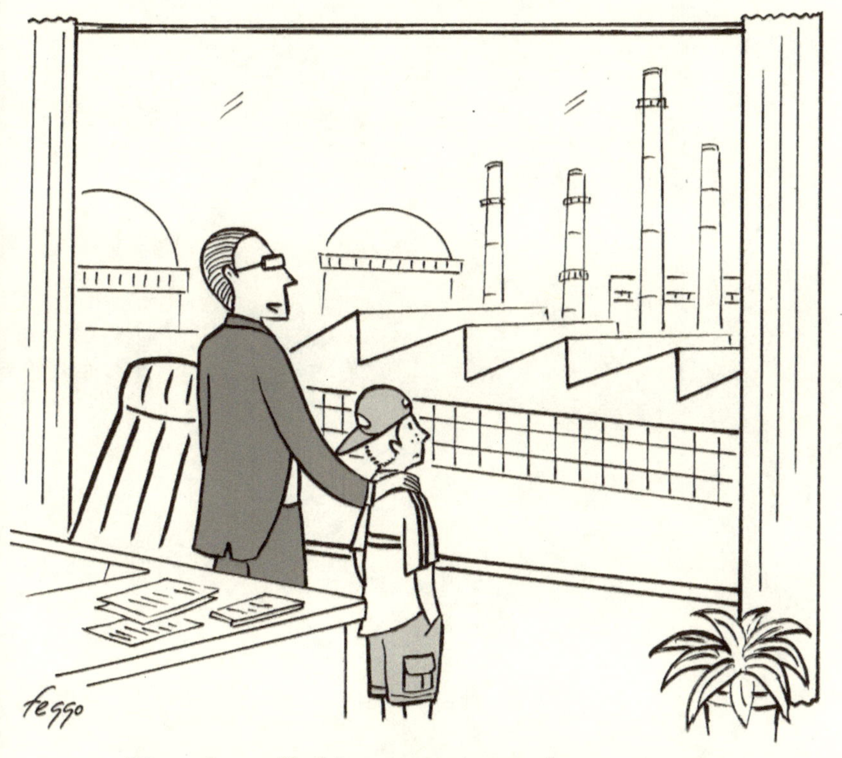

*"One day, all this was going to be yours, son.
Now, it's not even mine."*

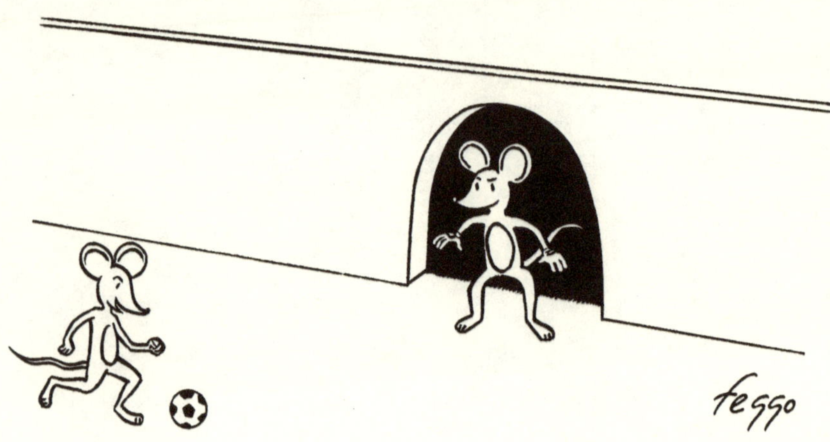
feggo

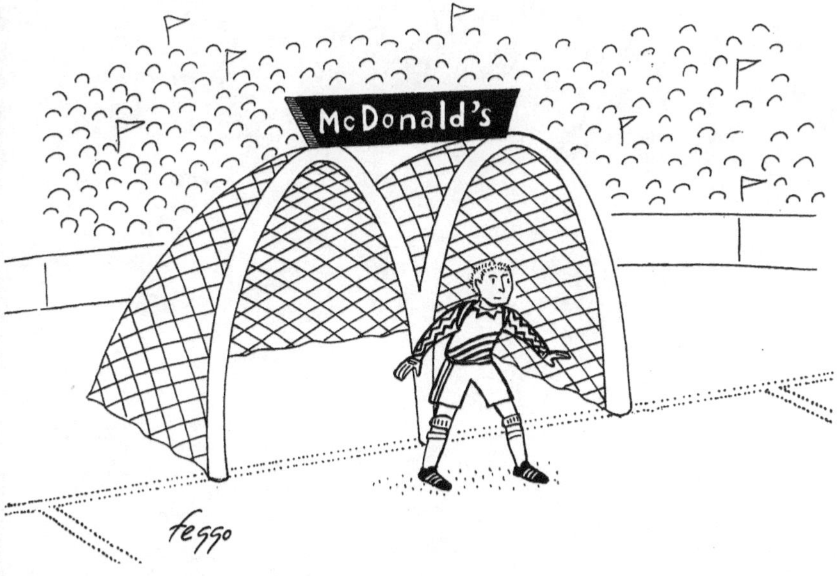
McDonald's
feggo

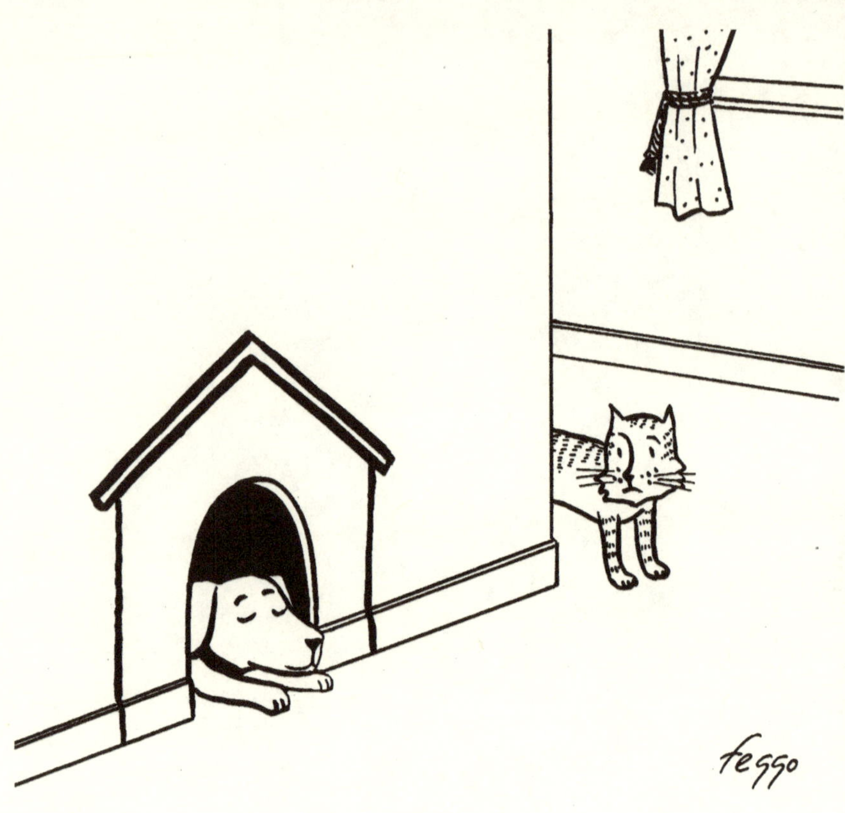
feggo

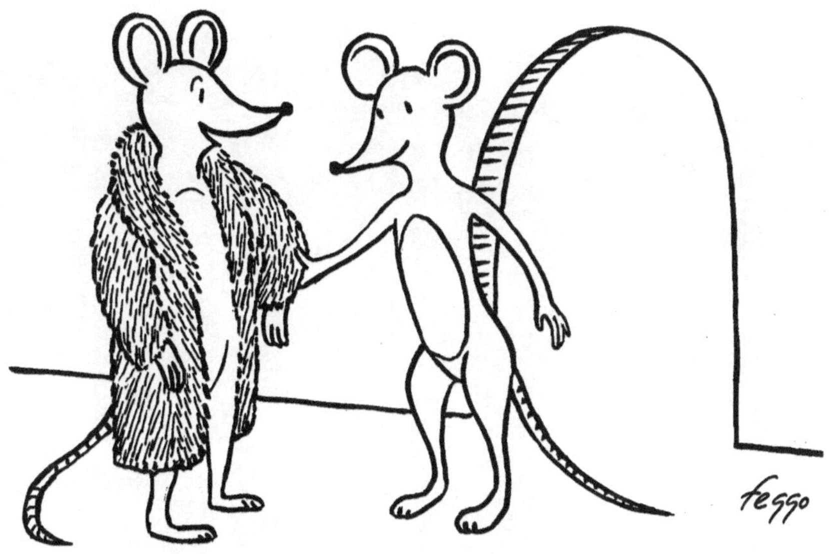

"It's made from authentic furballs."

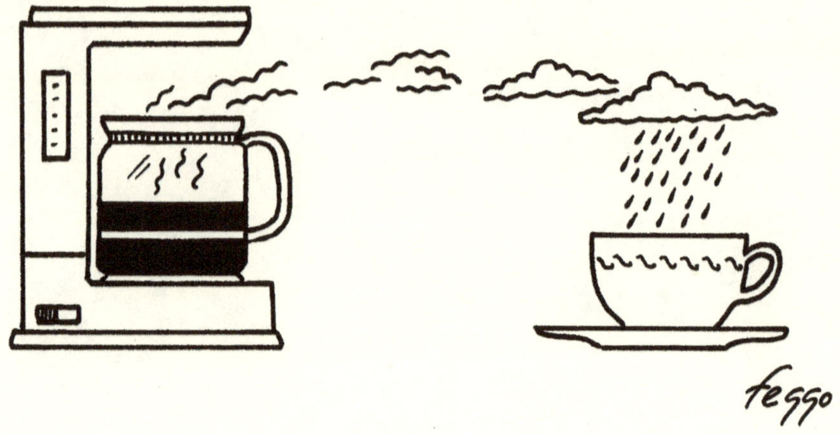

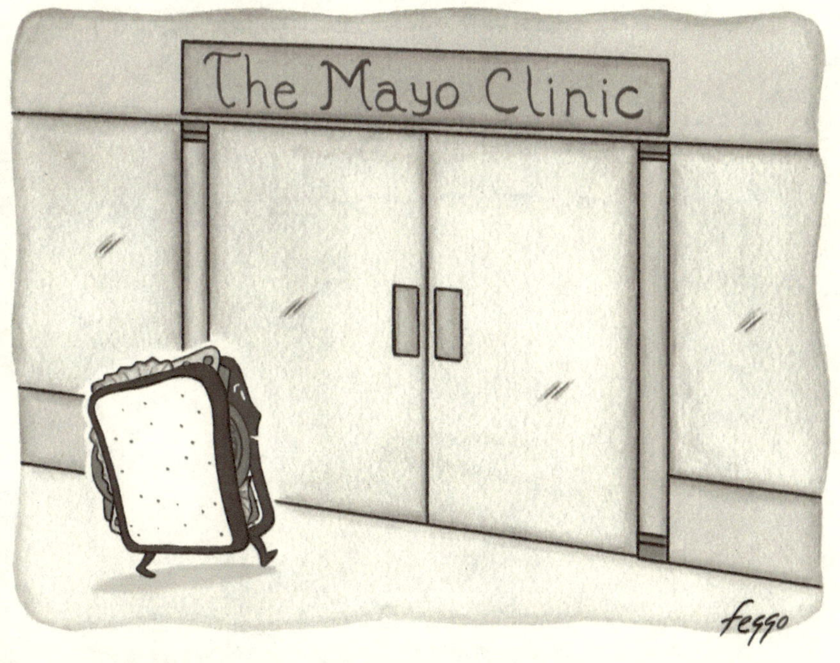
The Mayo Clinic
feggo

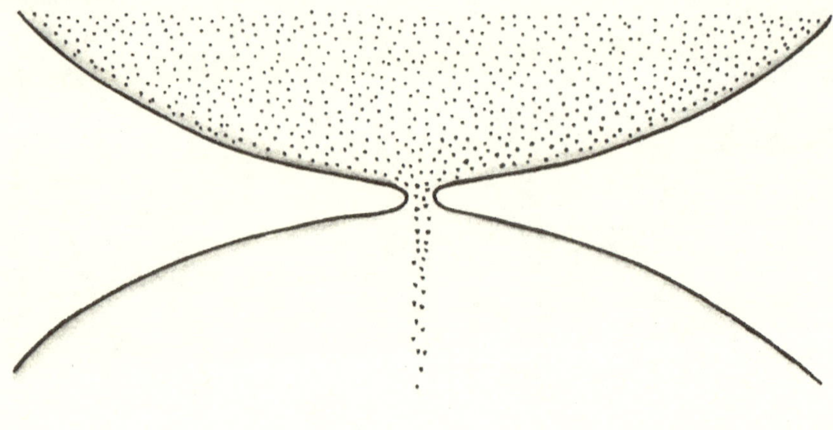

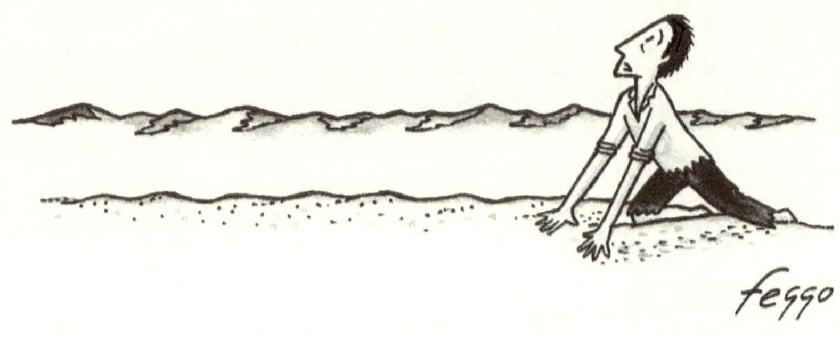
feggo

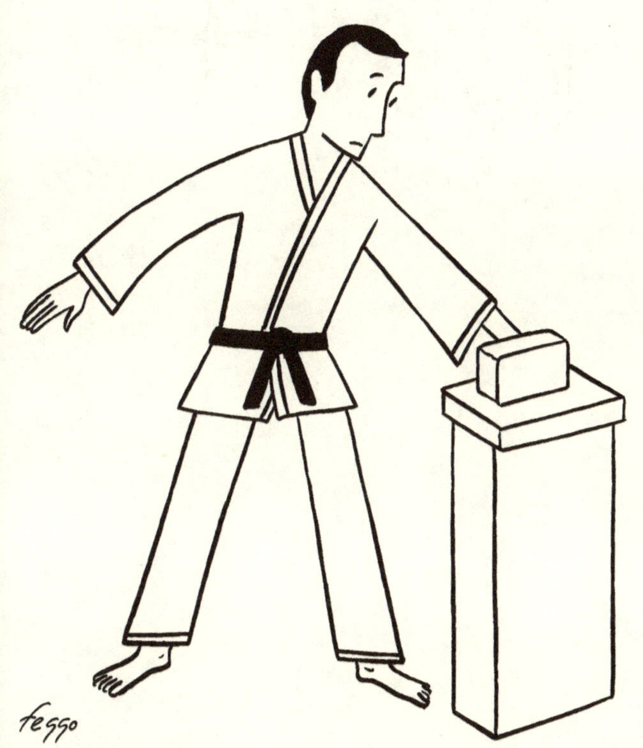

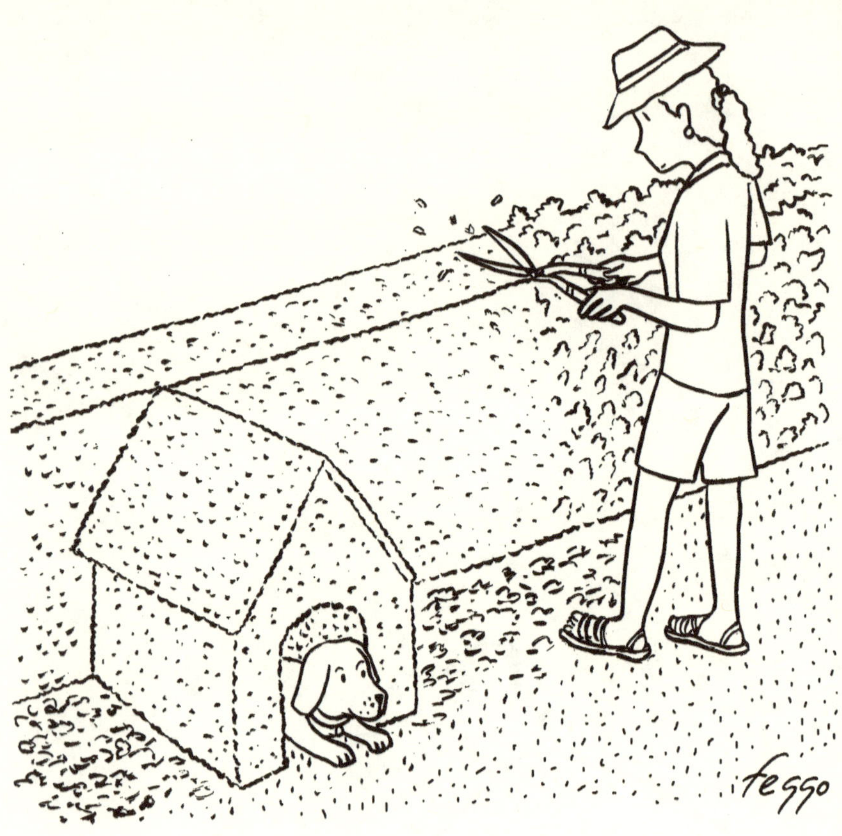
feggo

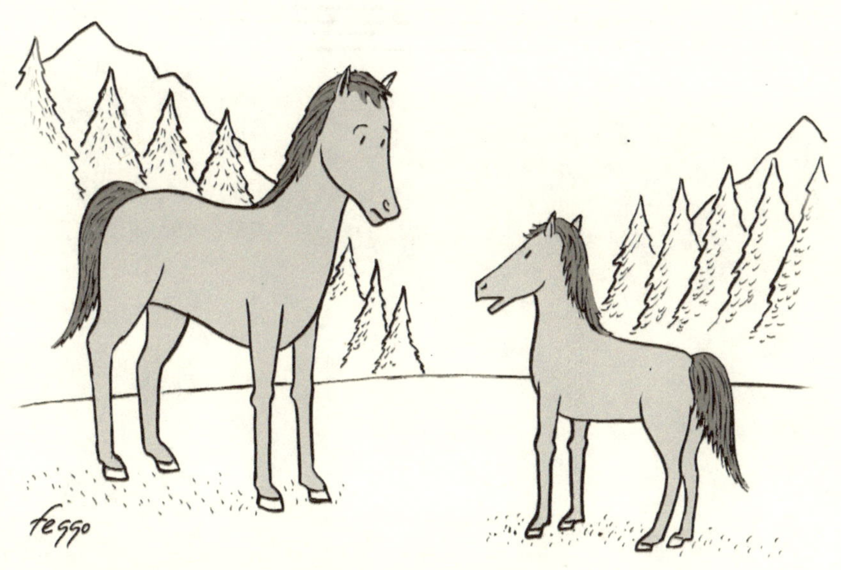

"When I grow up I want to be one of the Horses of the Apocalypse."

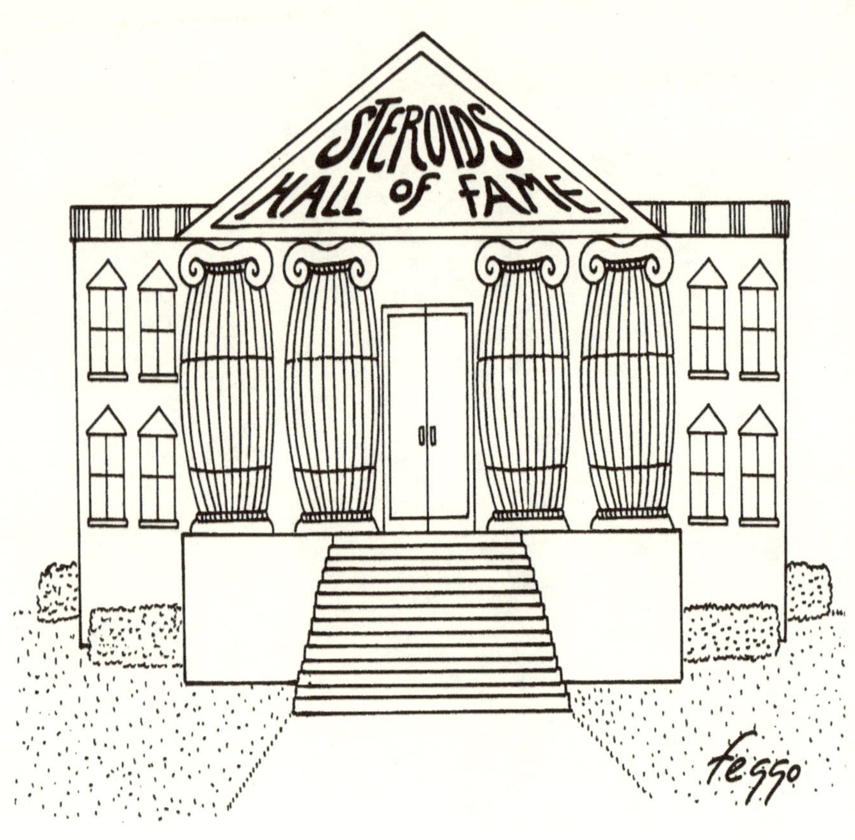
STEROIDS
HALL of FAME
fe.ggo

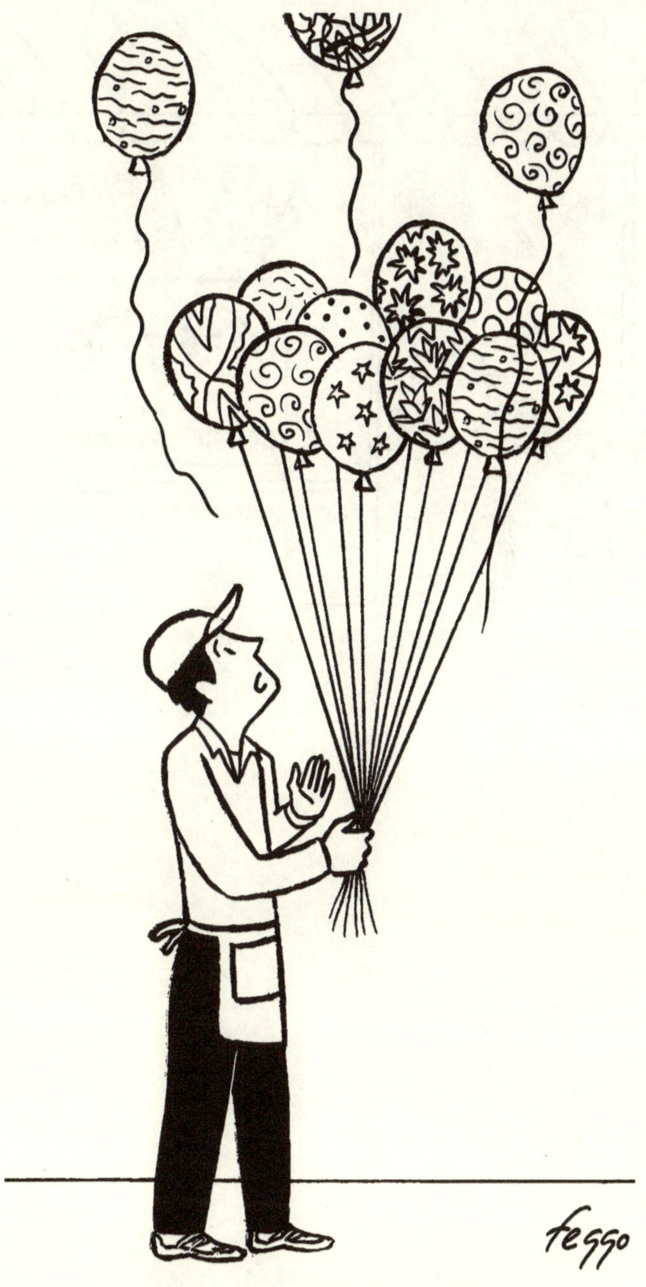

"Sorry guys, sales are slow. I'm going to have to let some of you go."

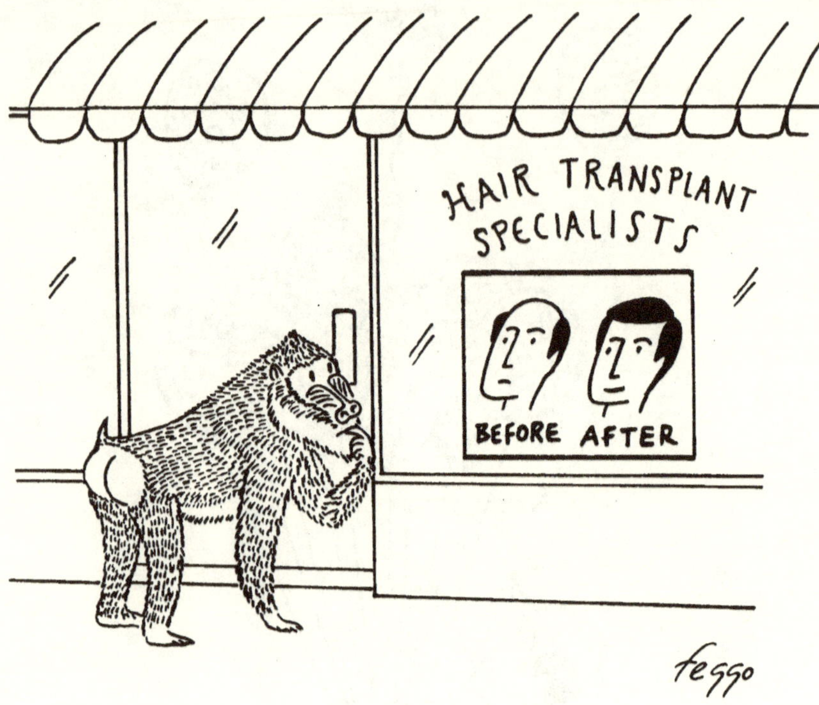
HAIR TRANSPLANT SPECIALISTS
BEFORE
AFTER
feggo

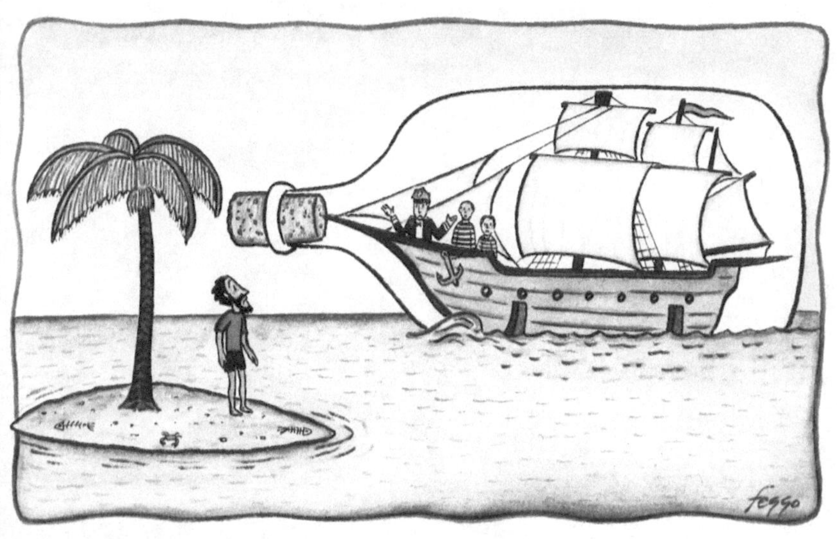
feggo

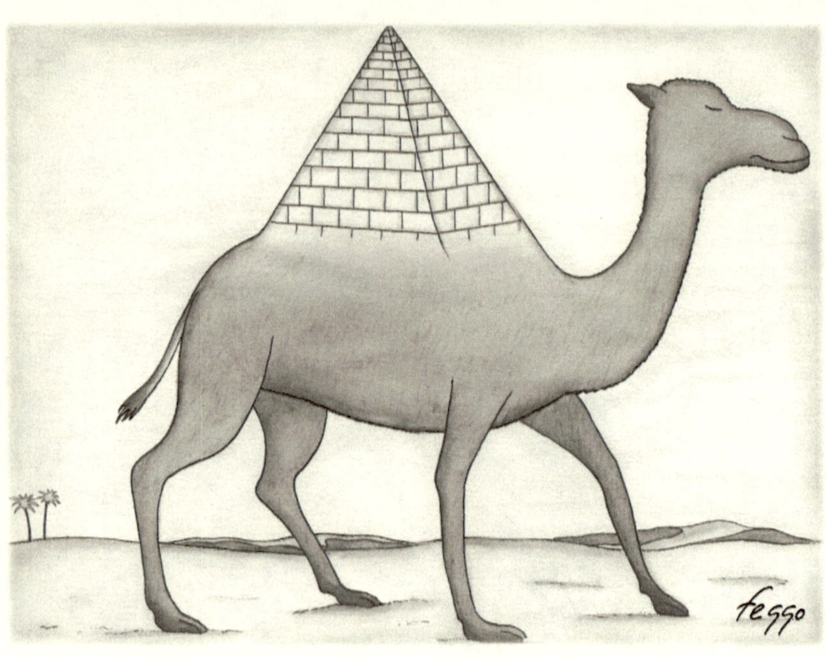
feggo

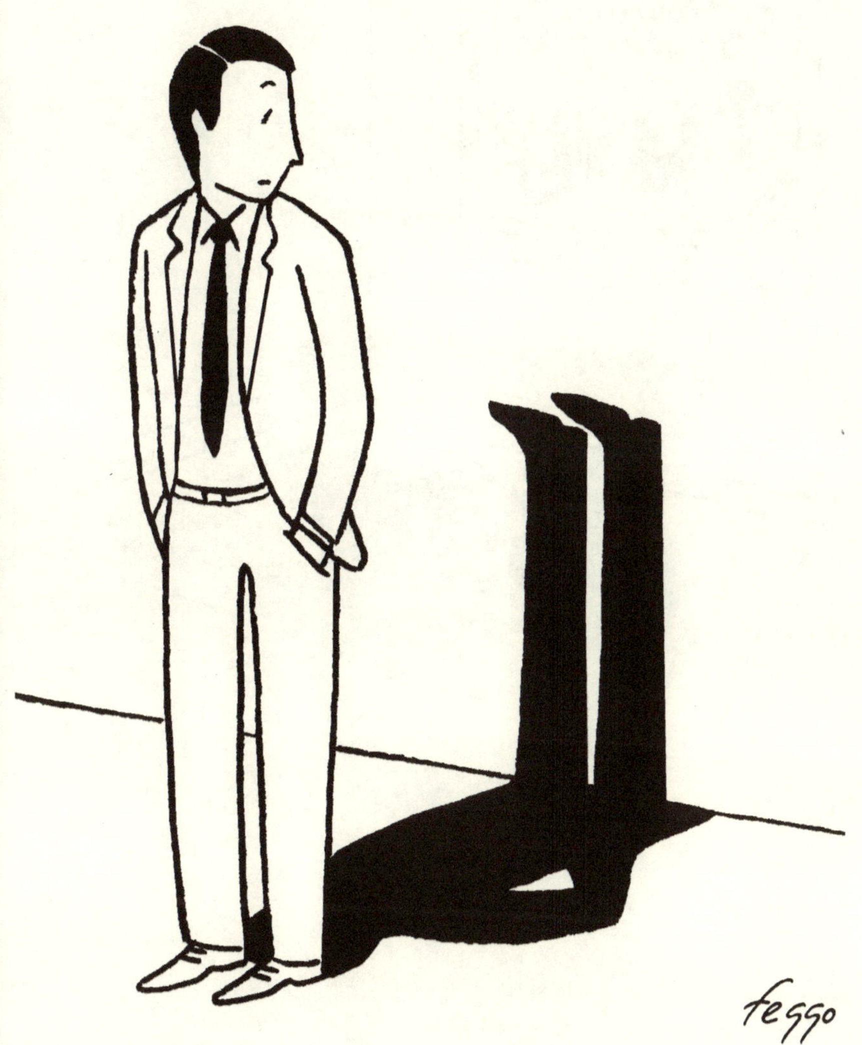
feggo

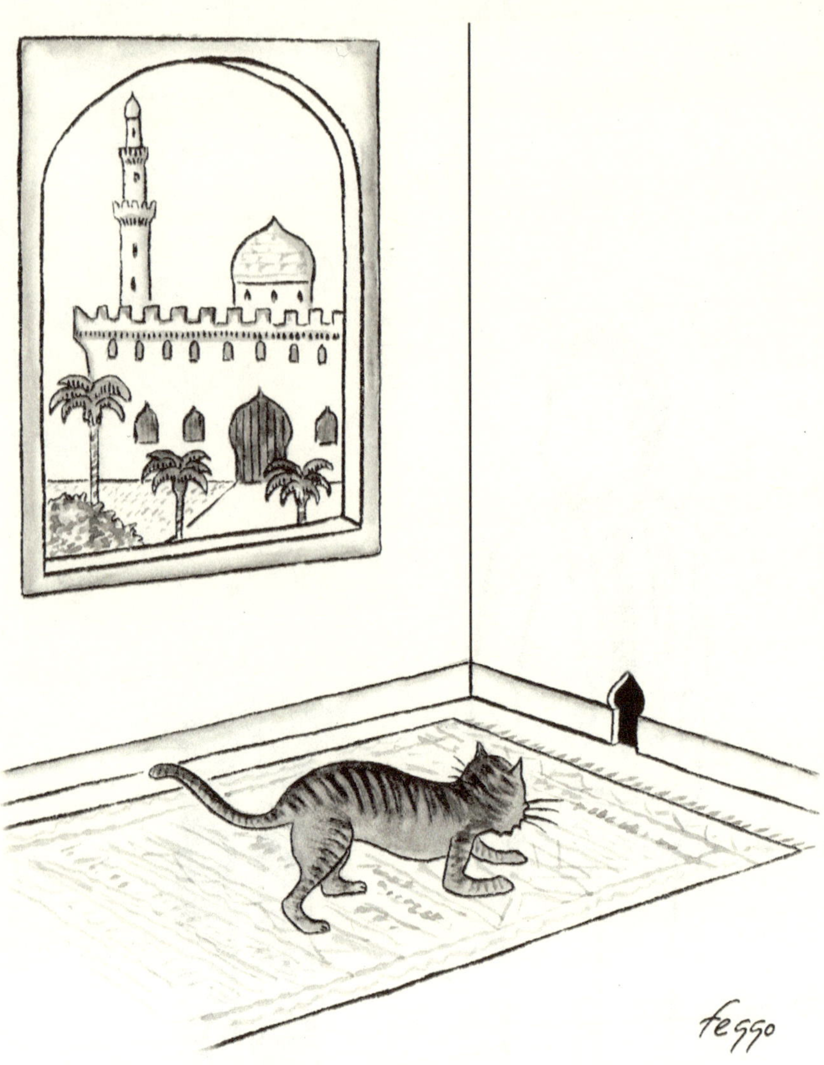
feggo

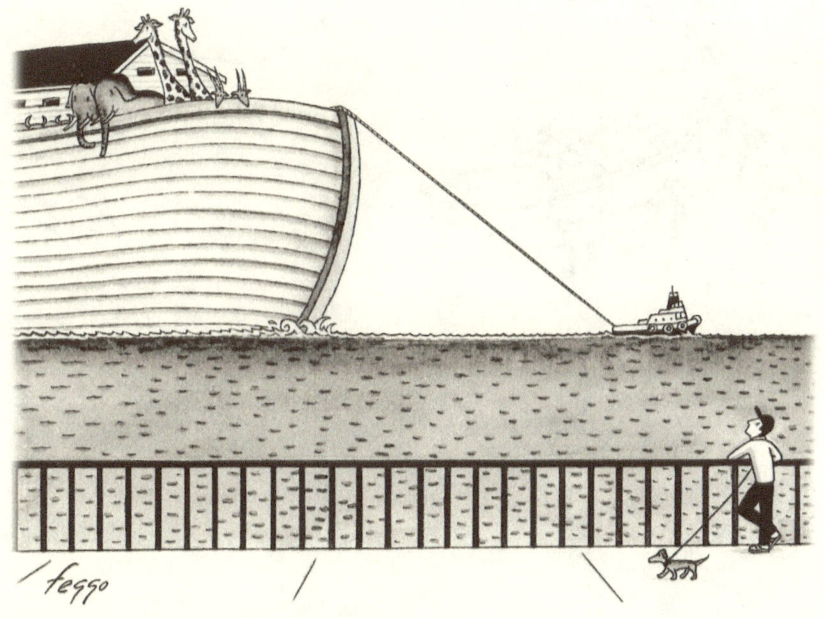
feggo

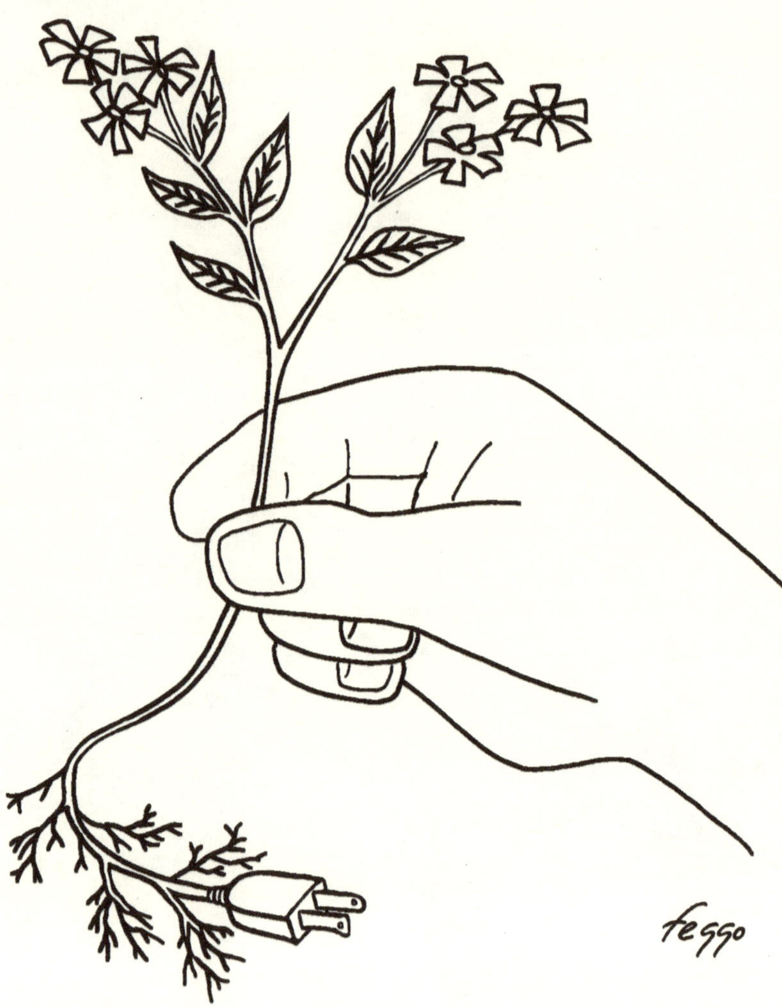
feggo

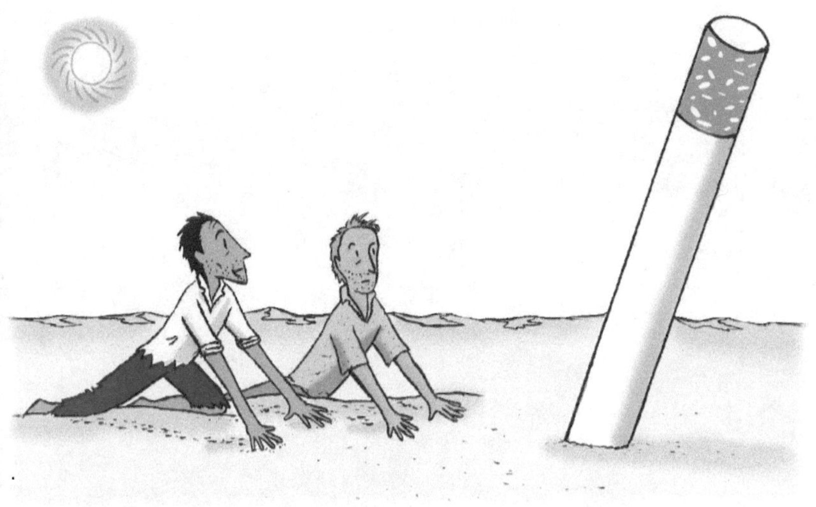

"Look, a camel!"

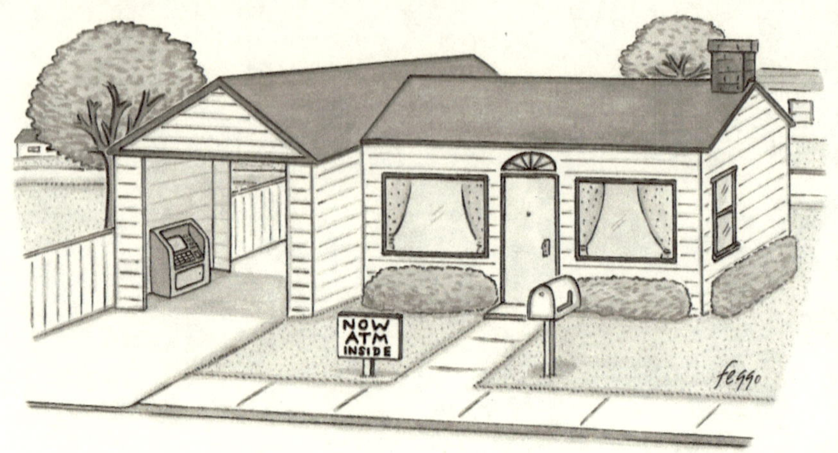
NOW
ATM
INSIDE
fegao

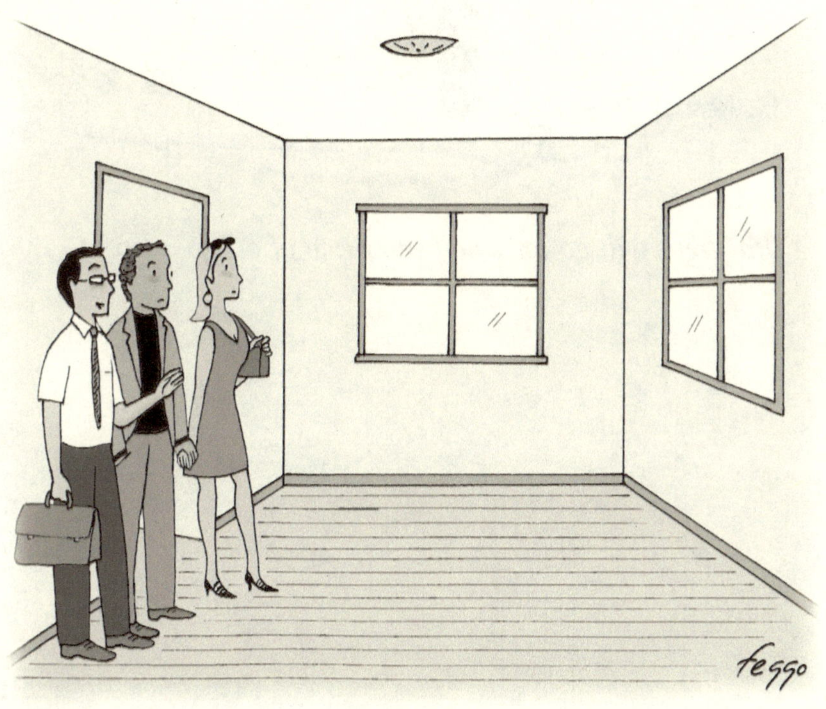

". . . and this is the room for error."

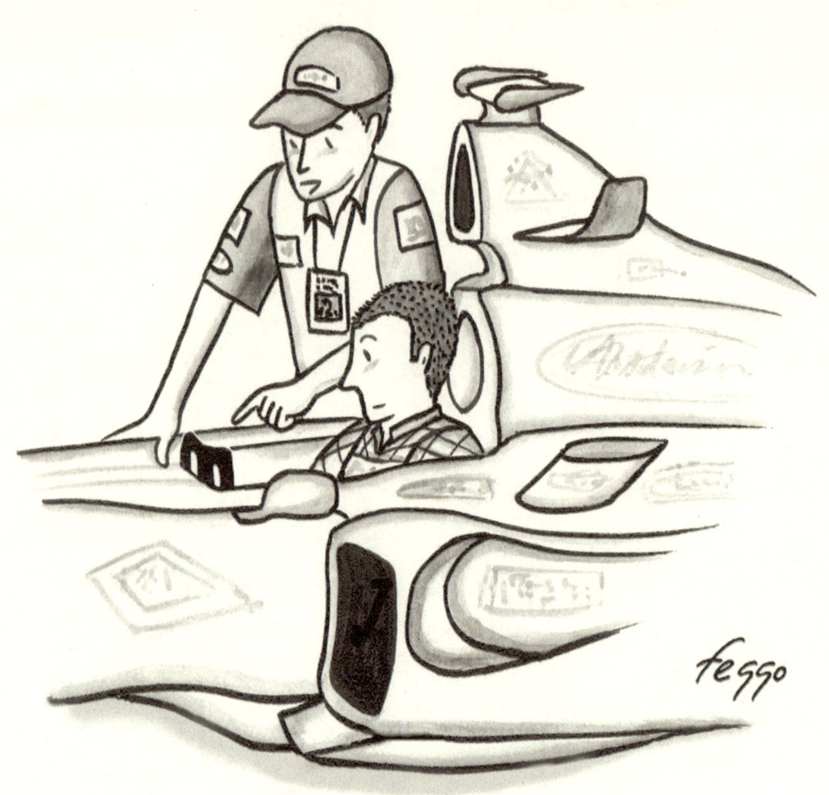

"That light will go on when the price of oil goes up."

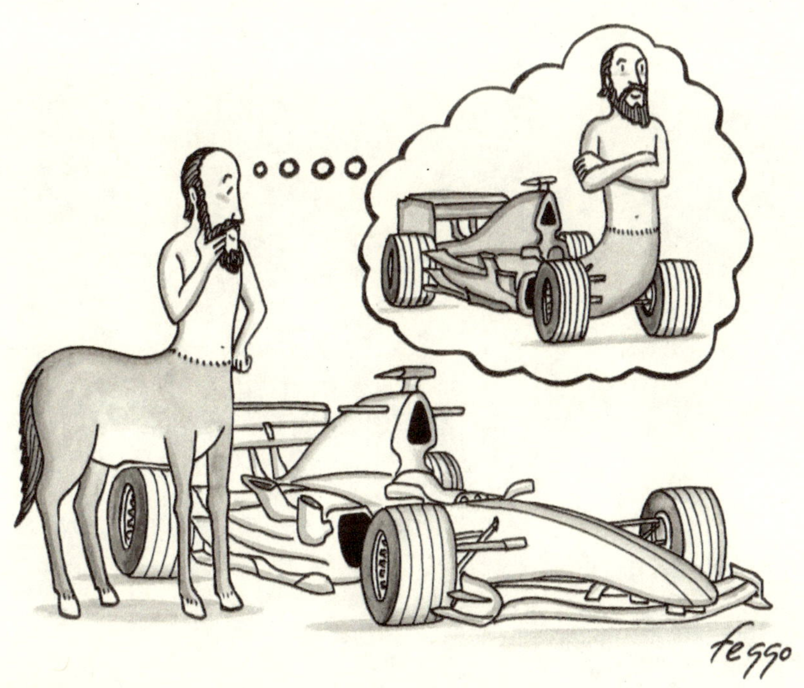
feggo

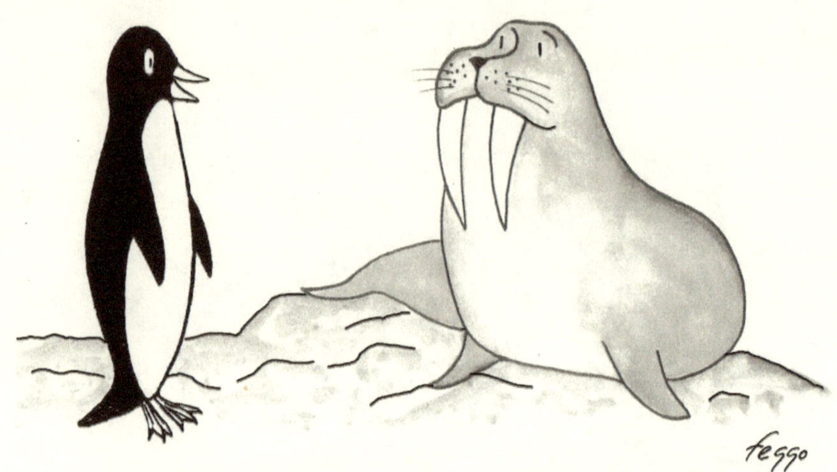

"My dad was white, my mom black."

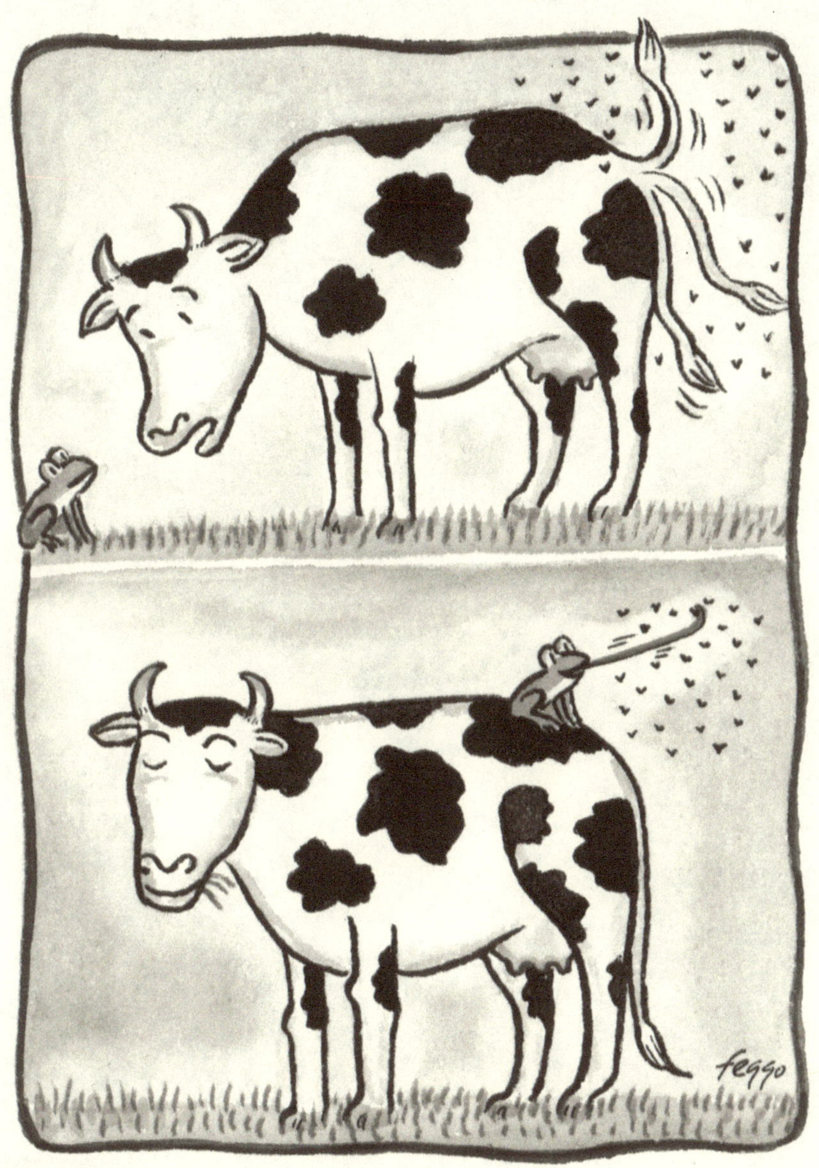
fegso

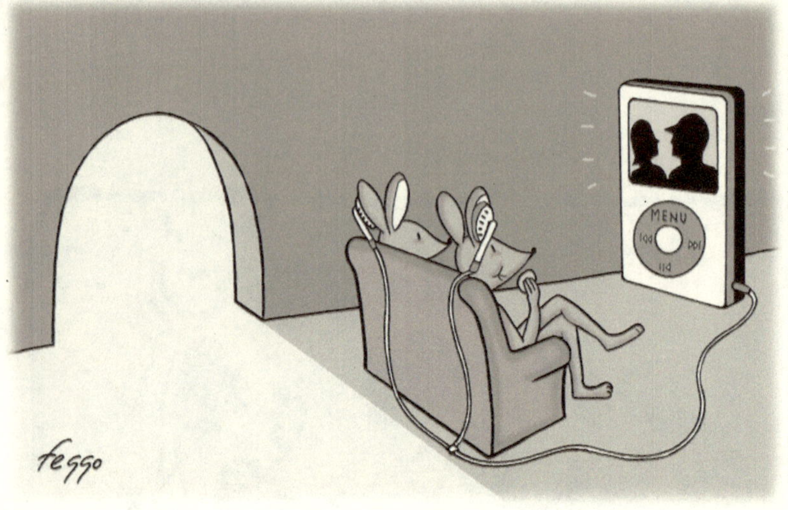
MENU
feggo

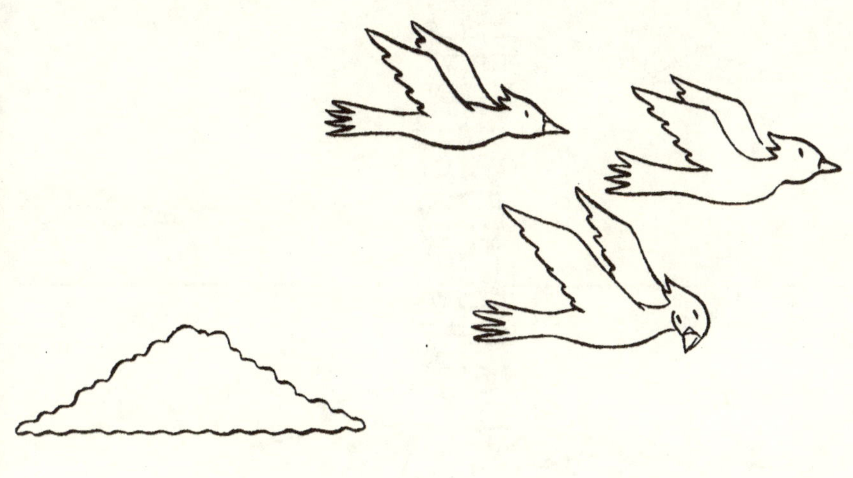

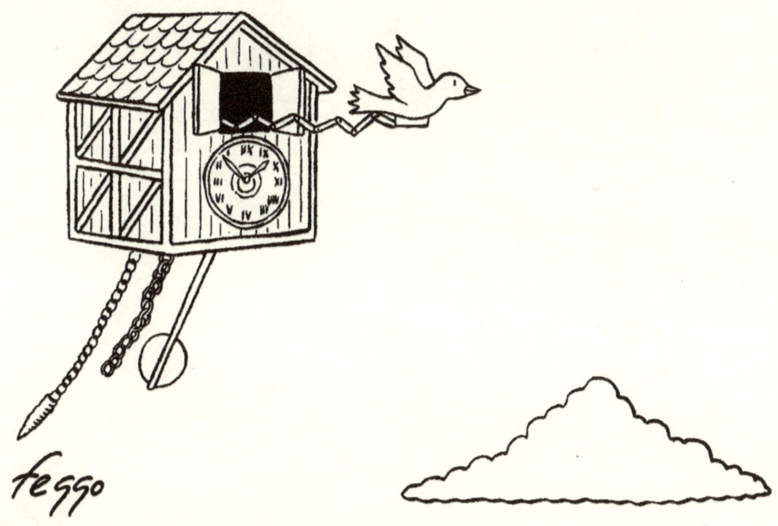
feggo

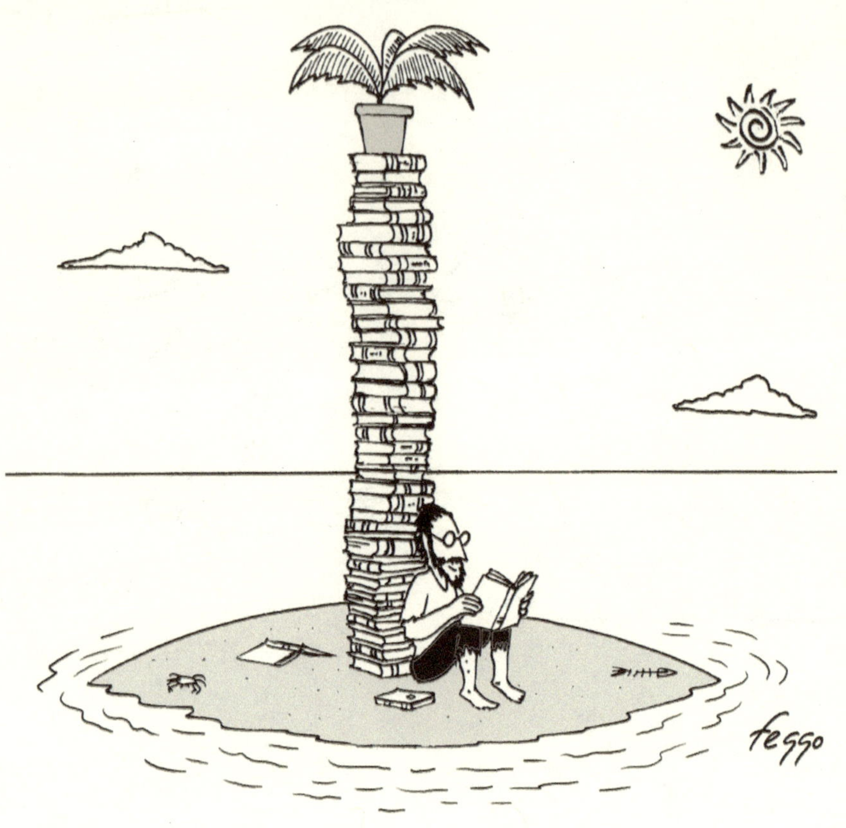
feggo

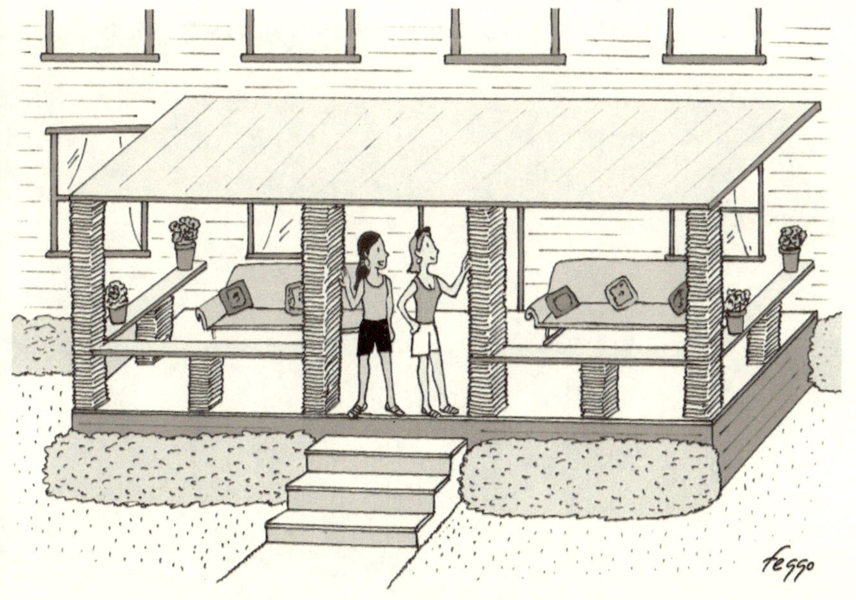

"These columns are my husband's rejected manuscripts."

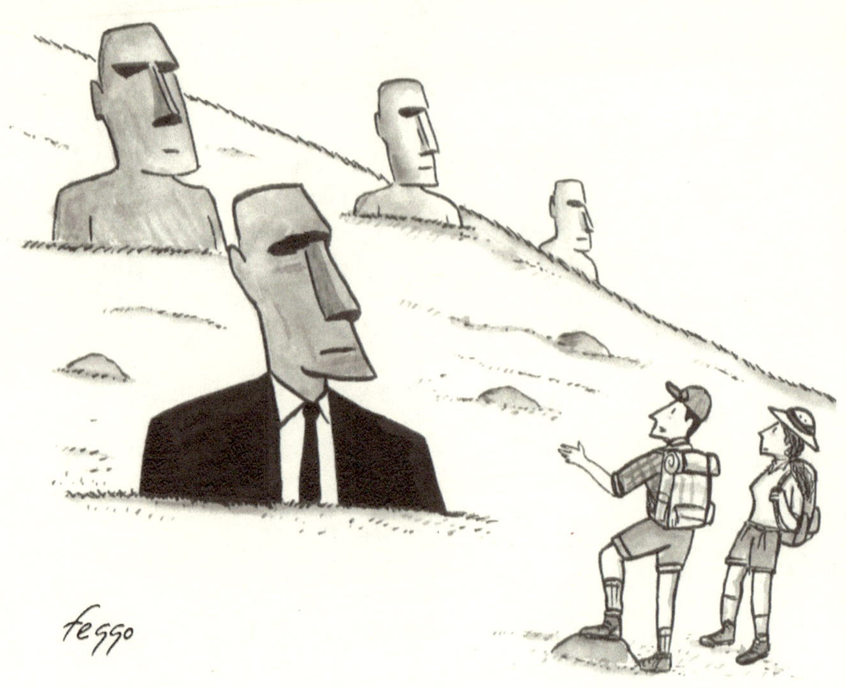

"At this point the Western influence starts to show."

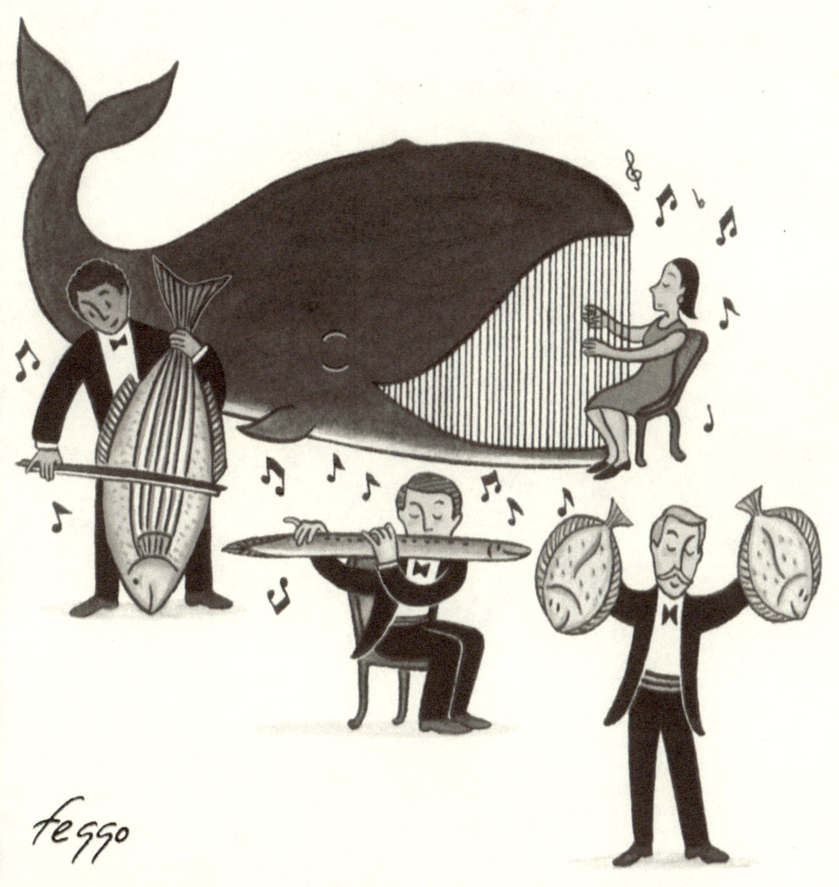
feggo

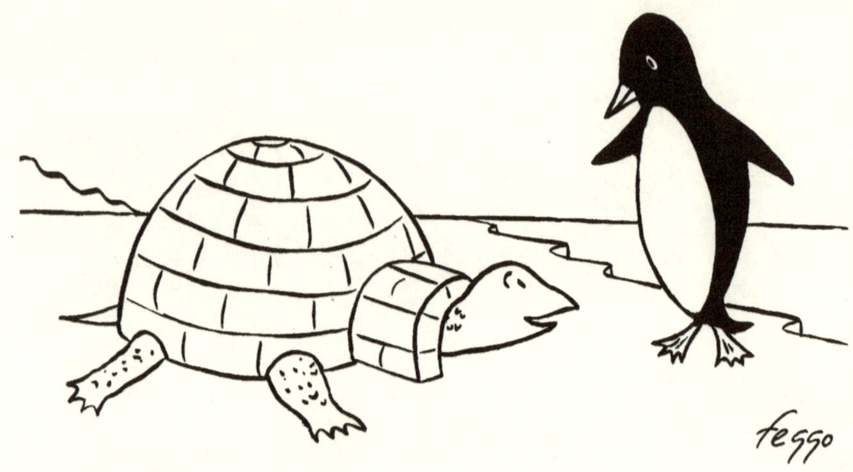

"It's a summer rental."

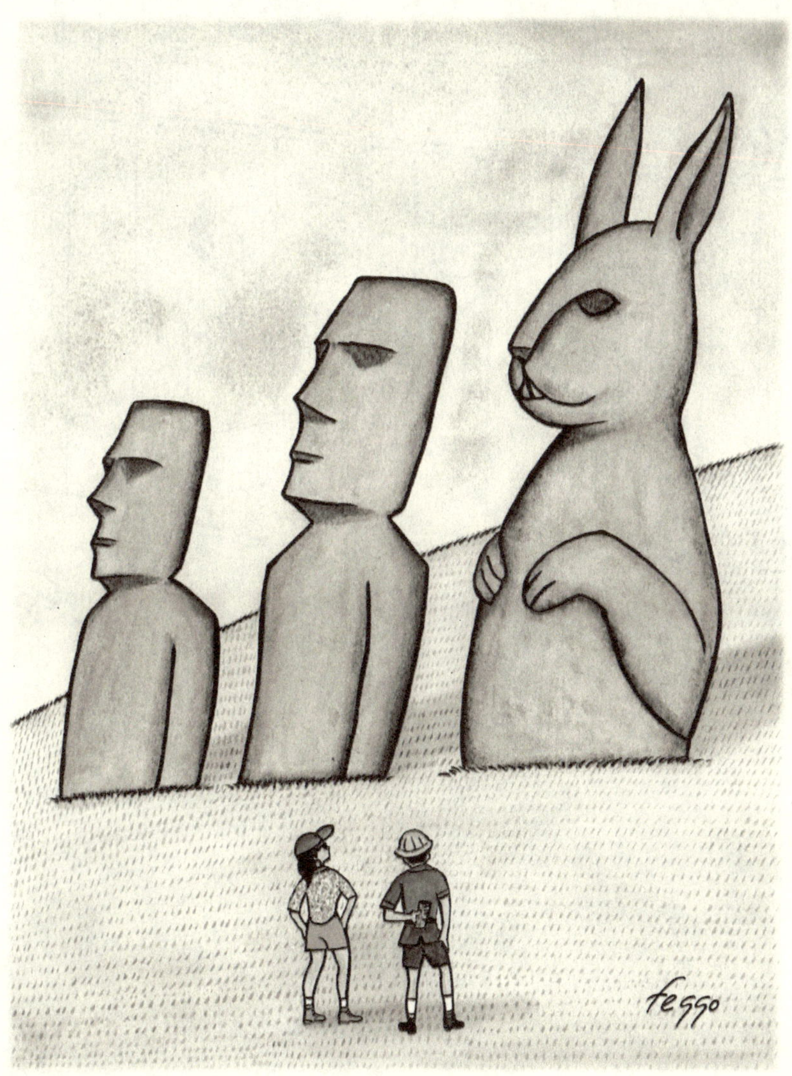
feggo

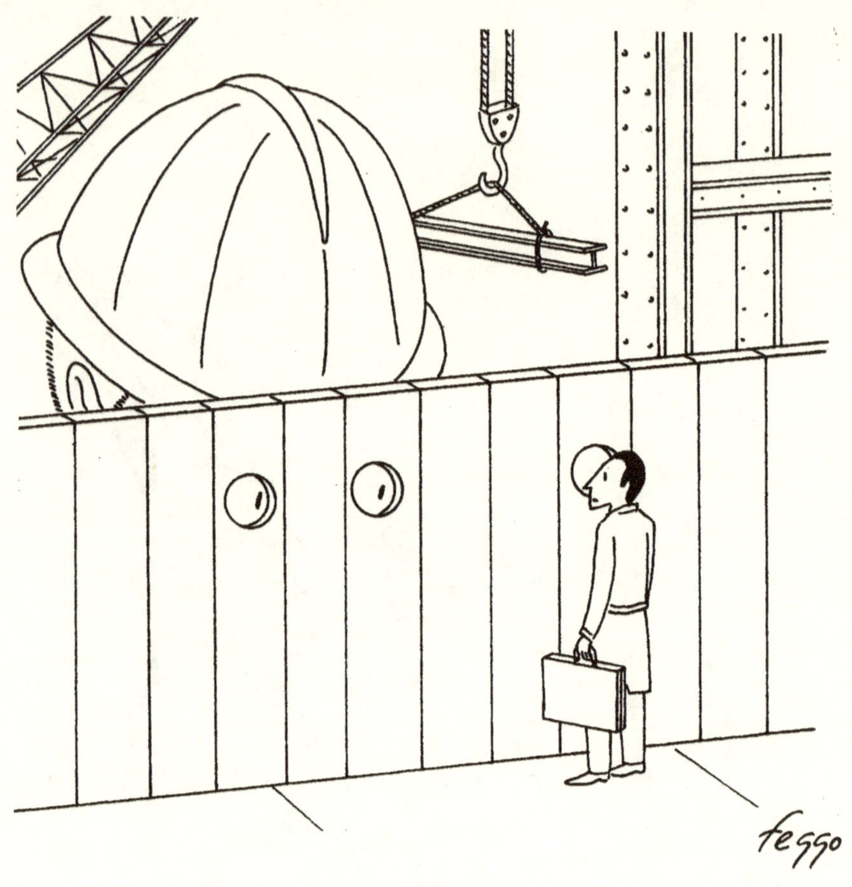
feggo

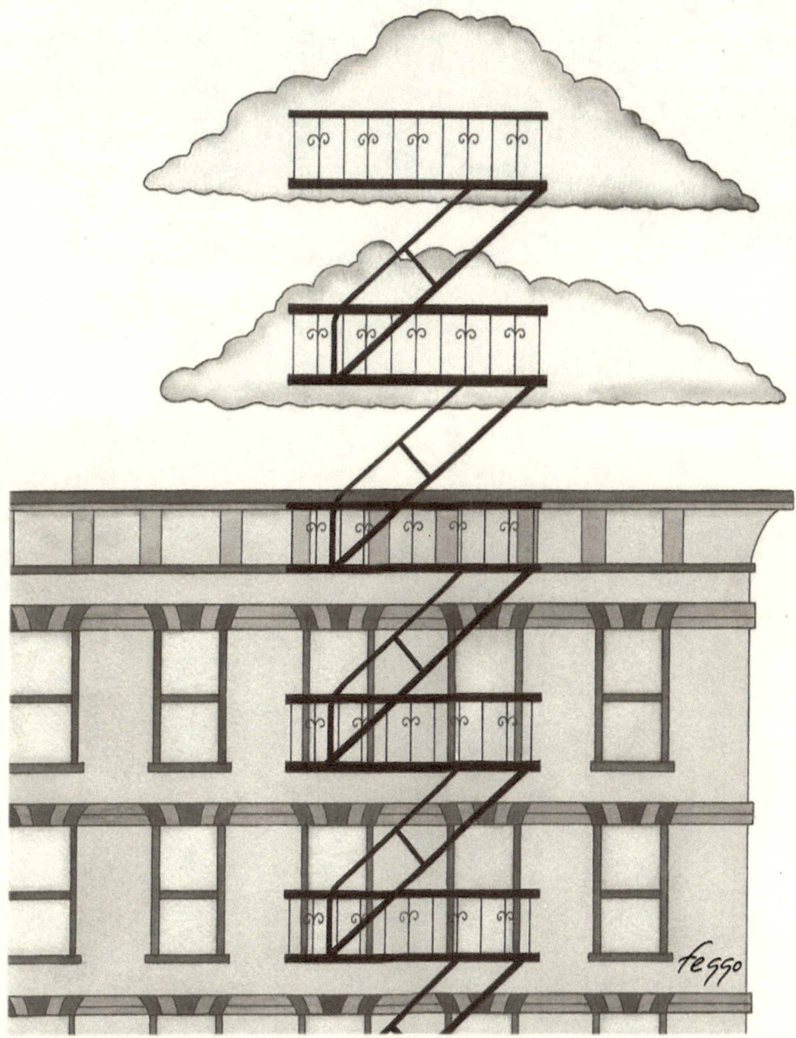
feggo

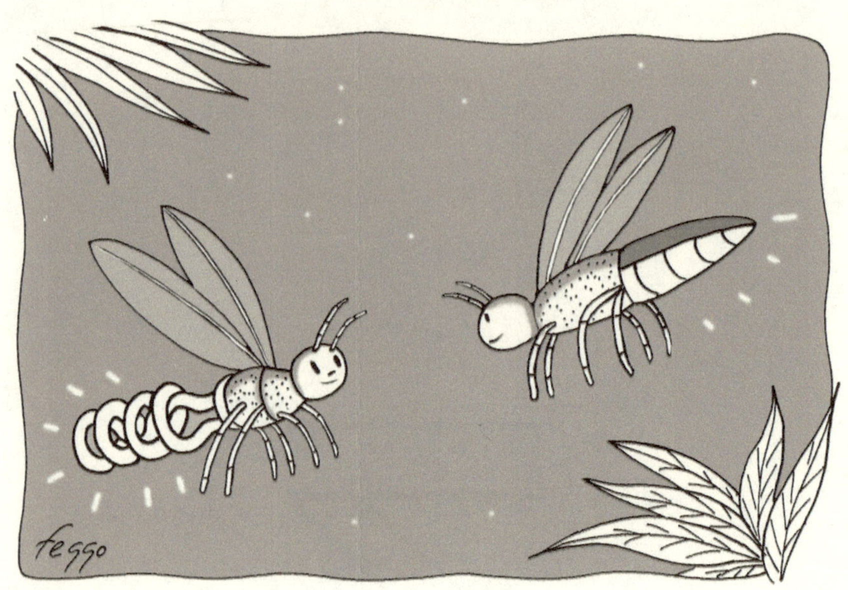
feggo

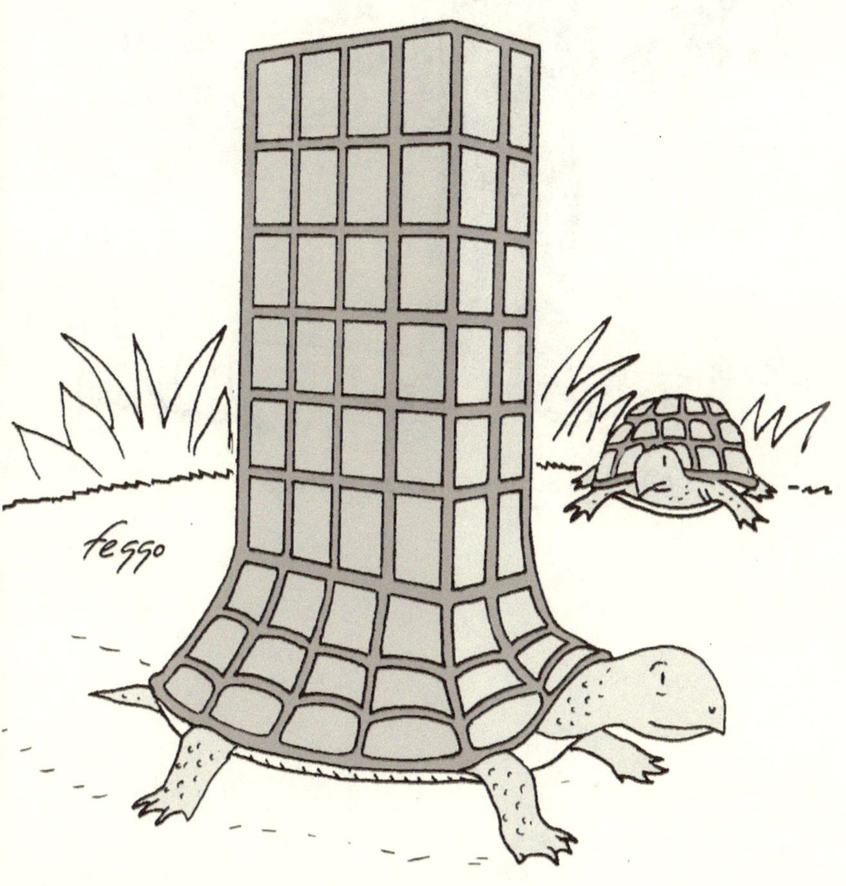
feggo

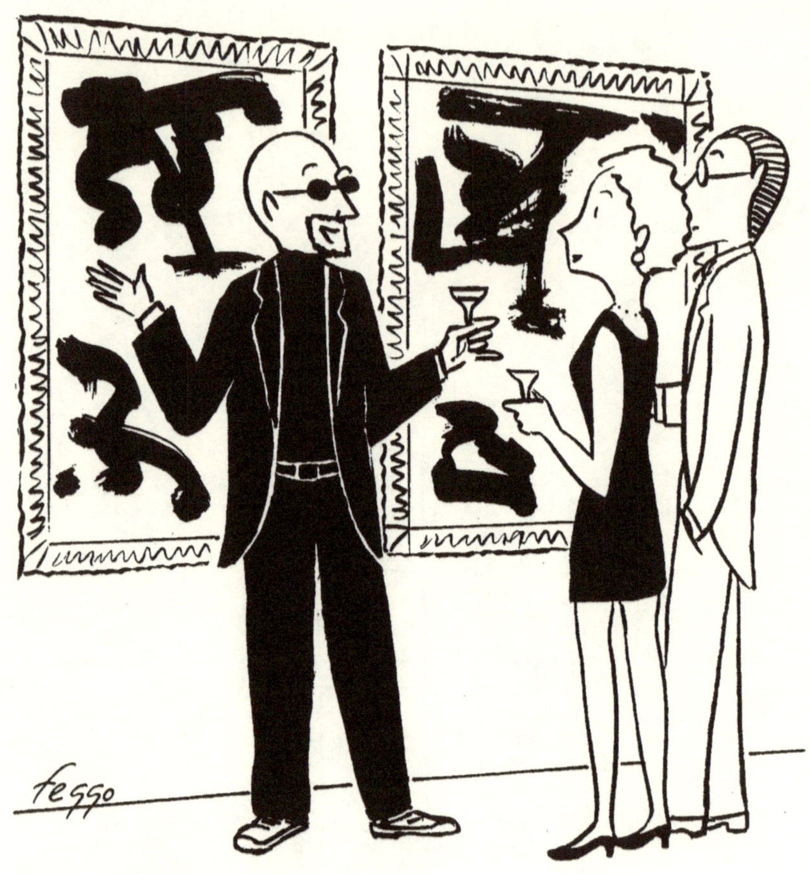

"I paint to support my brokerage services."

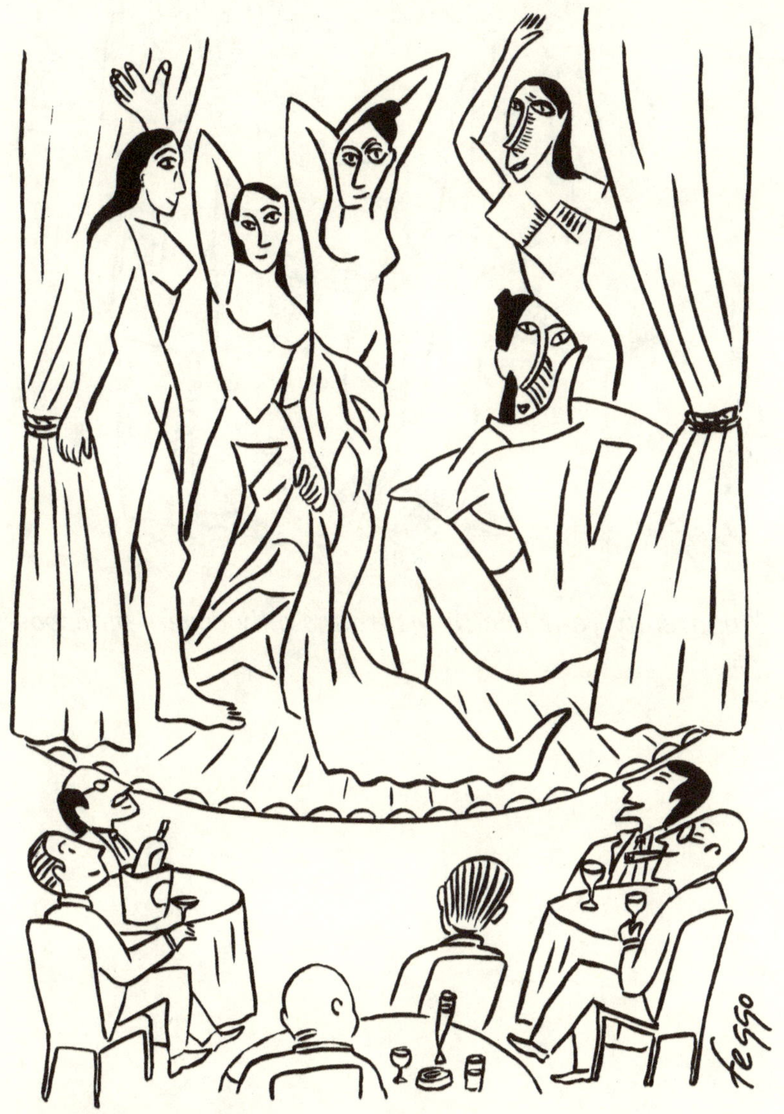
teggo

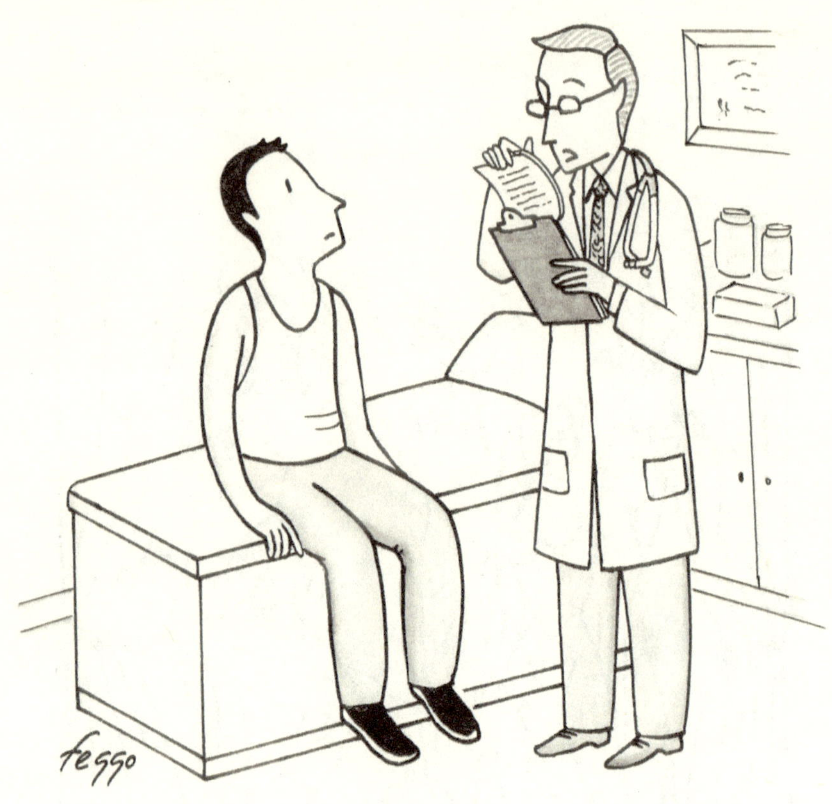

"Apparently your health insurance only covers placebos."

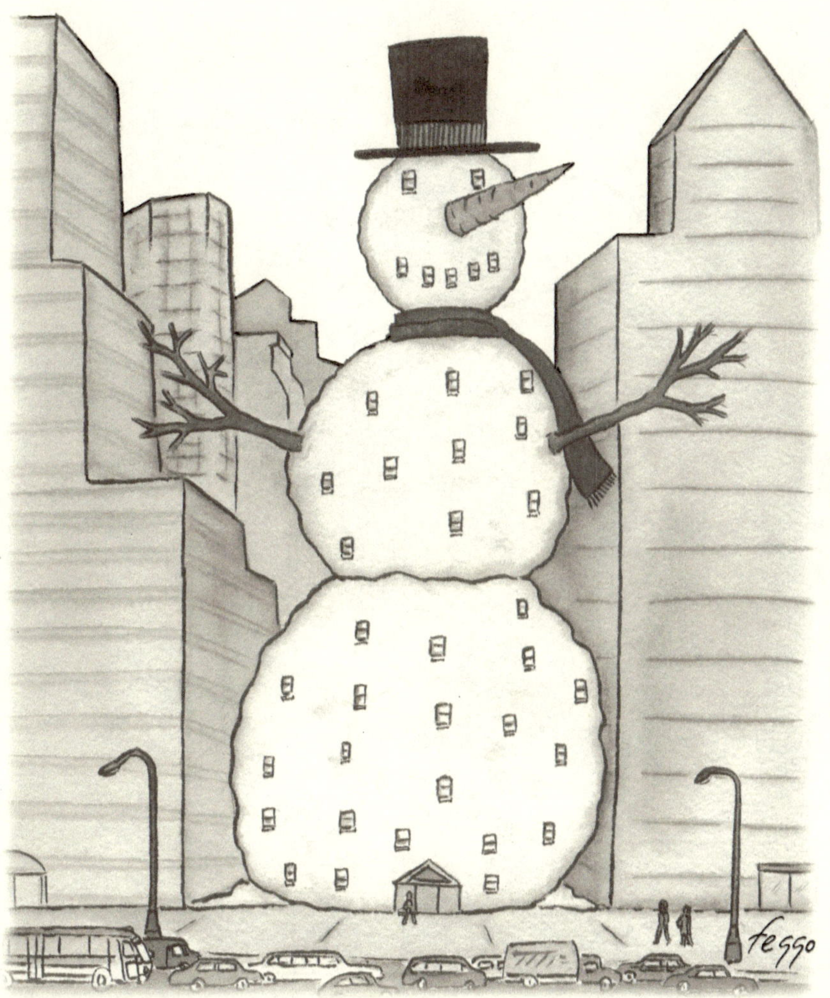
feggo

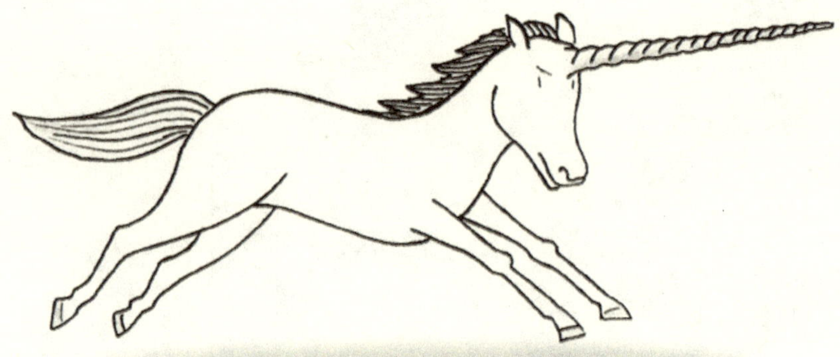

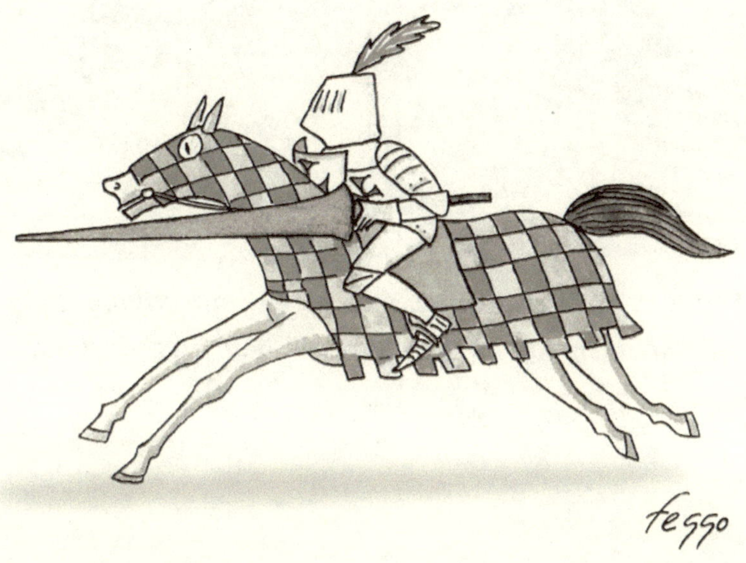
feggo

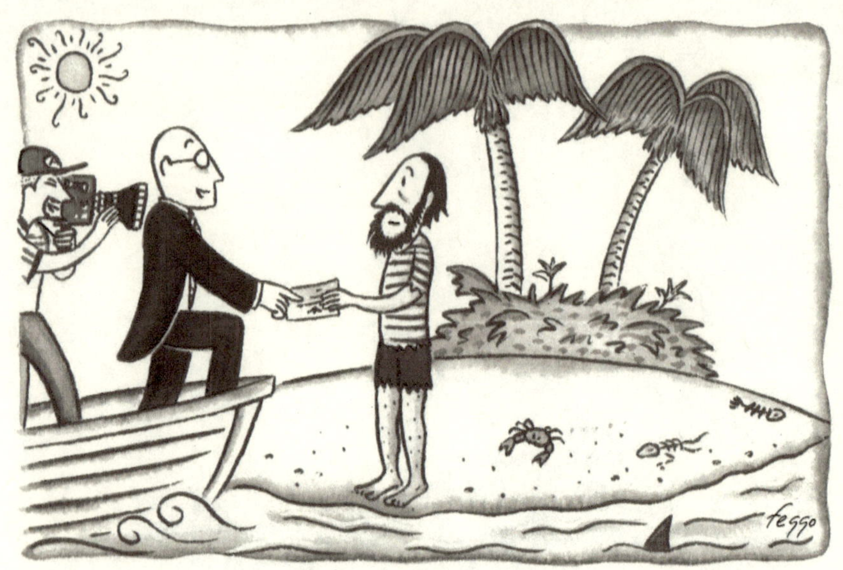

"You won the Survivor contest, here's your million dollars. Remember, you have to spend it here on the island."

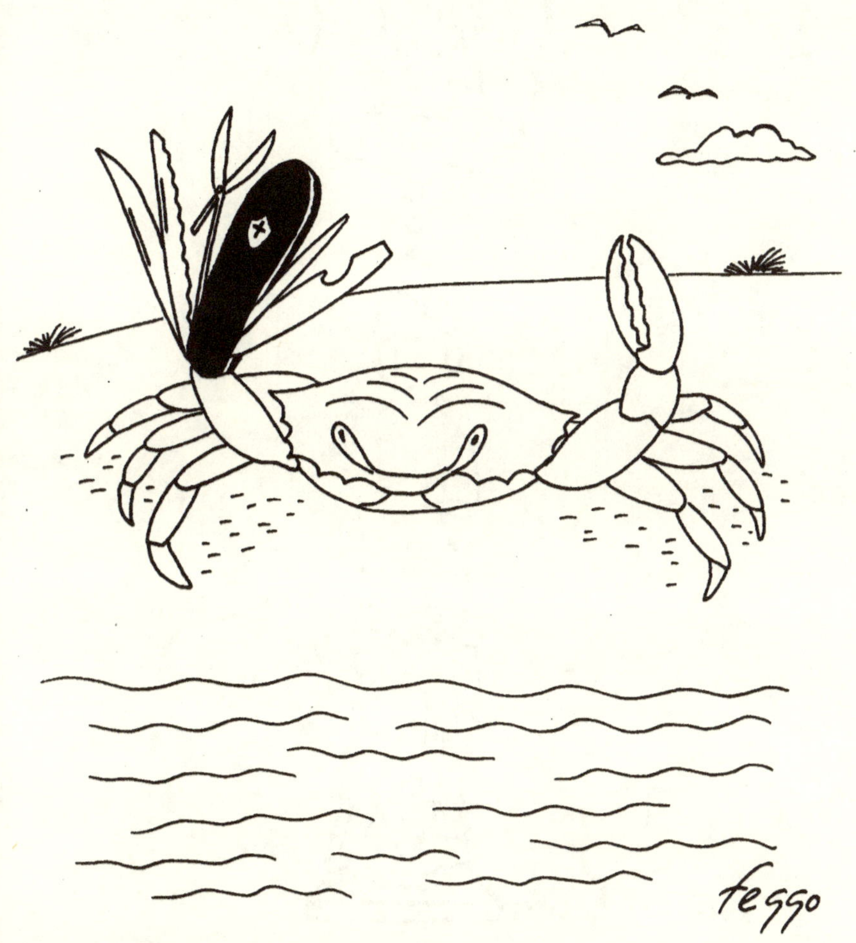
feggo

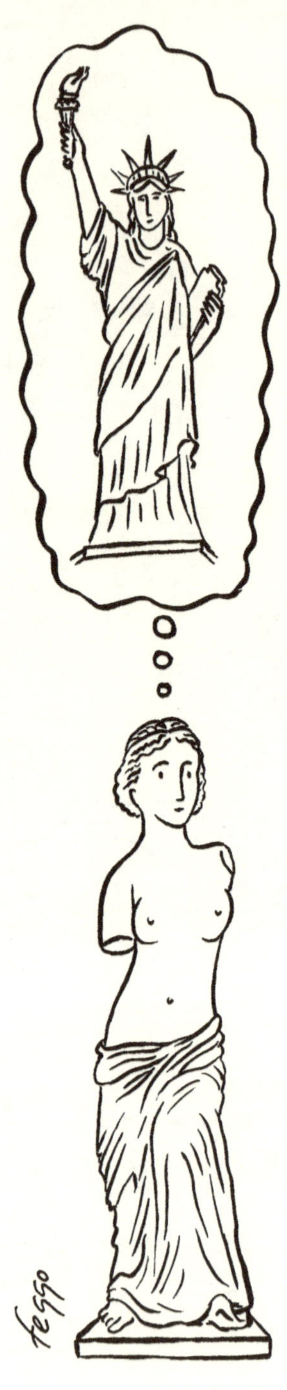
feggo

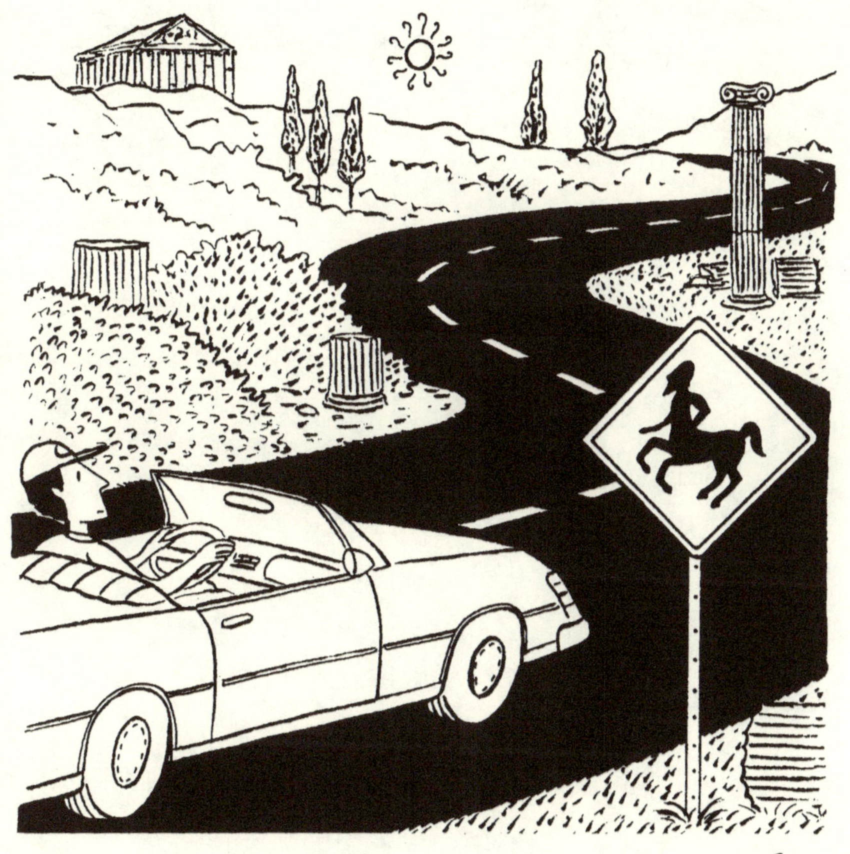
feggo

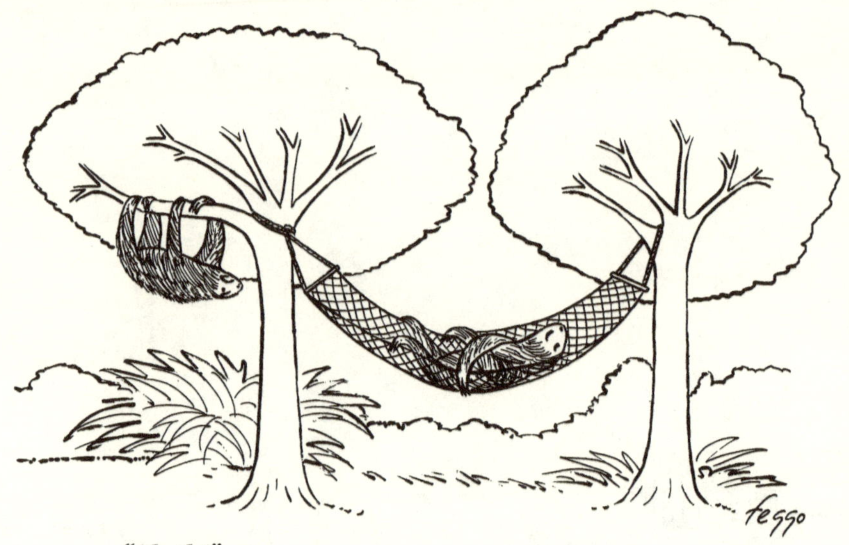

"Sloth!"

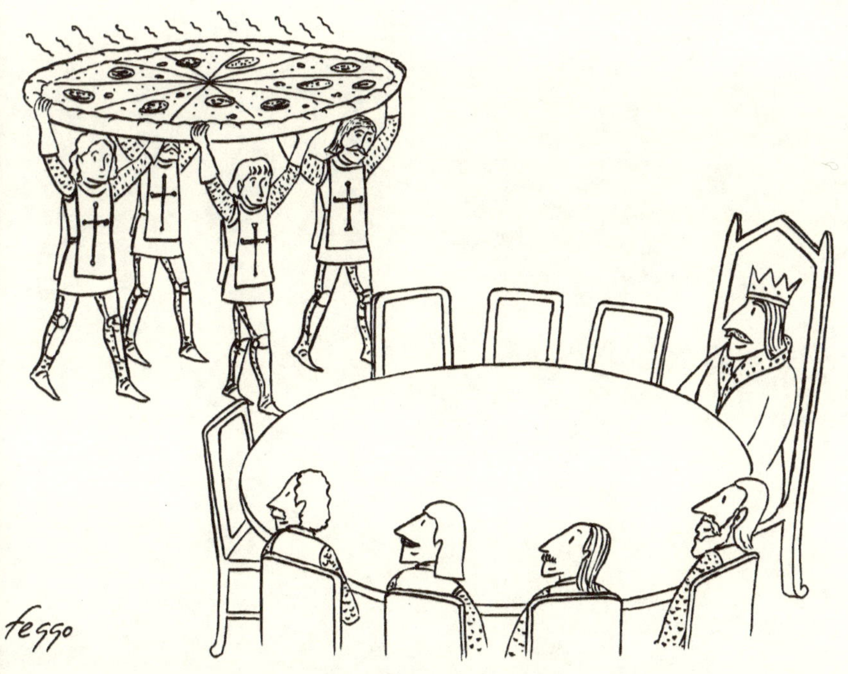
feggo

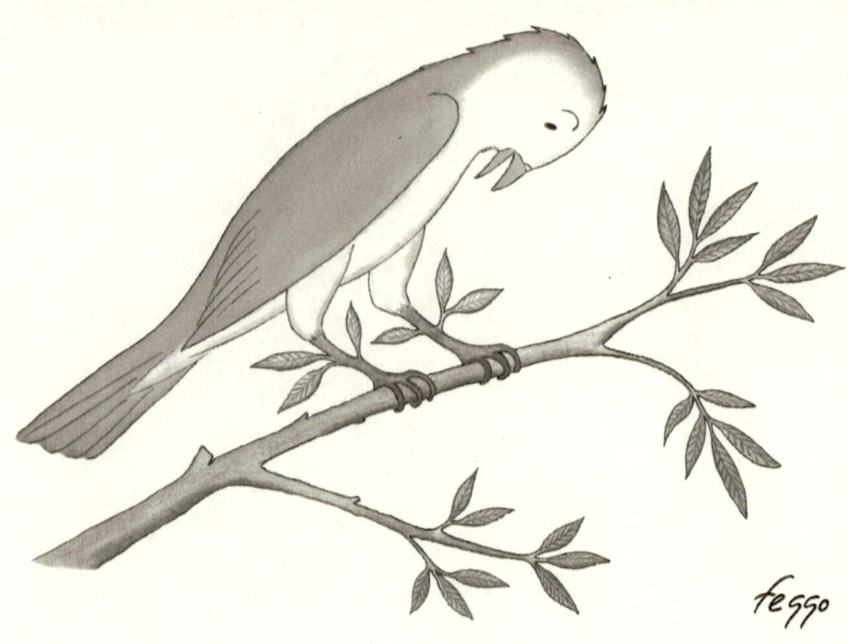
feggo

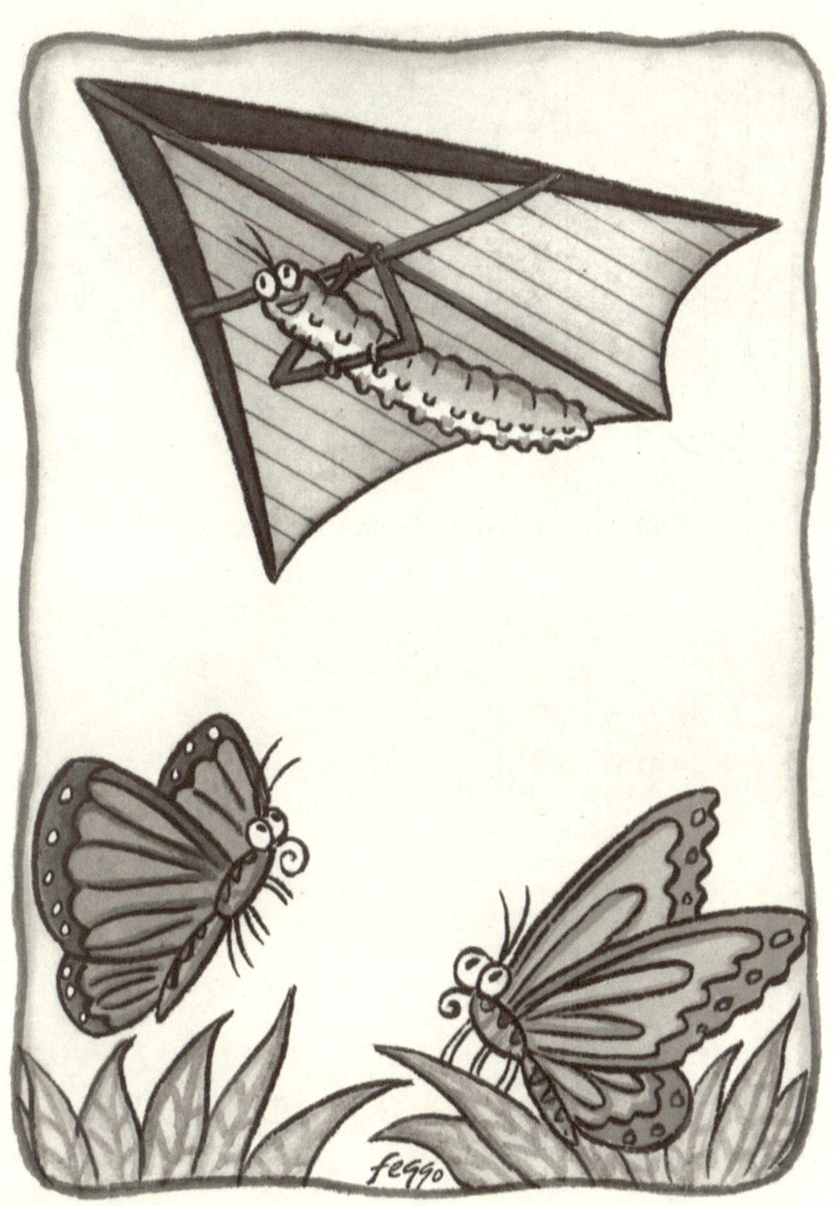
feggo

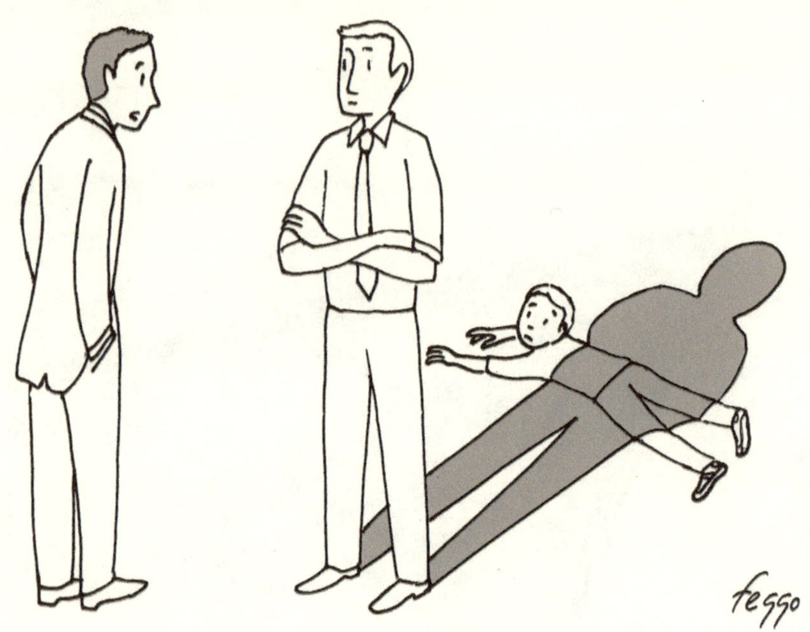

"You cast a heavy shadow on your son."

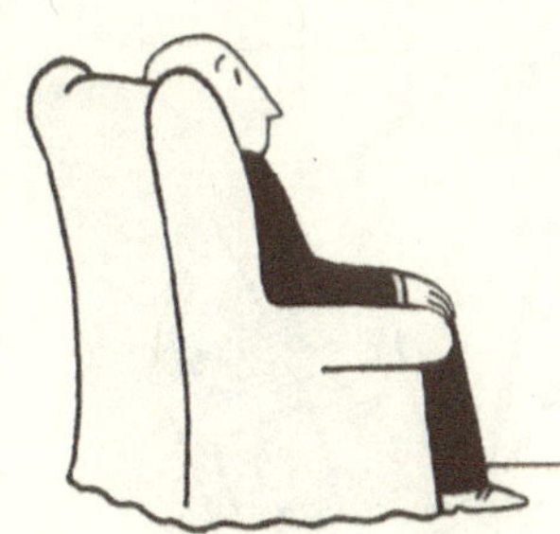
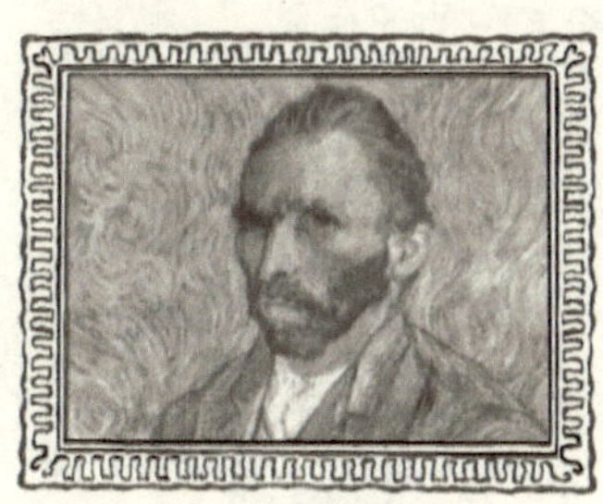
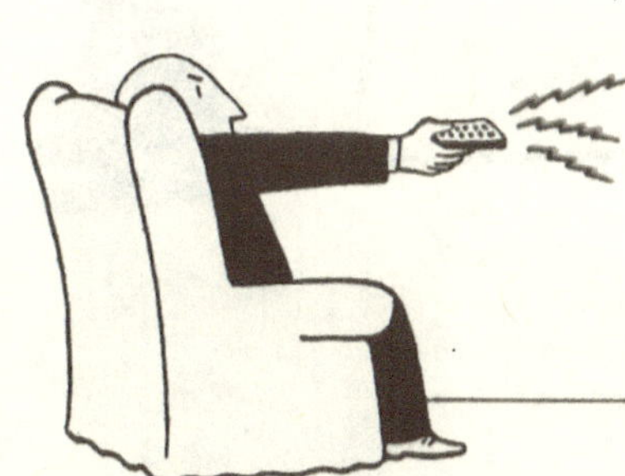
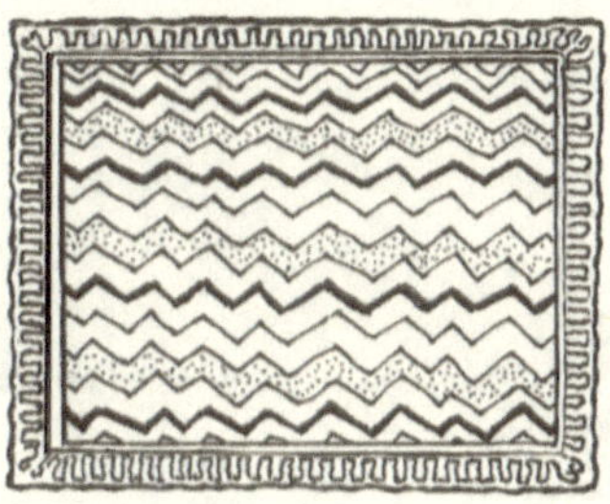
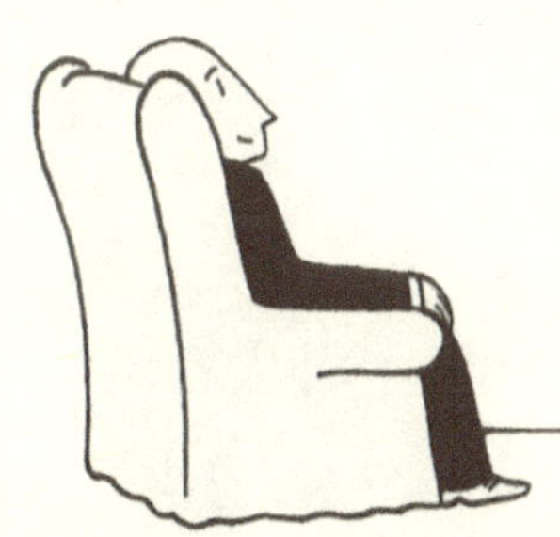
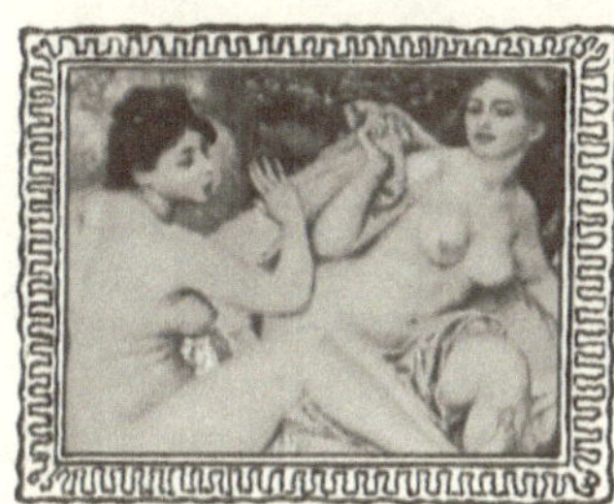

feggo

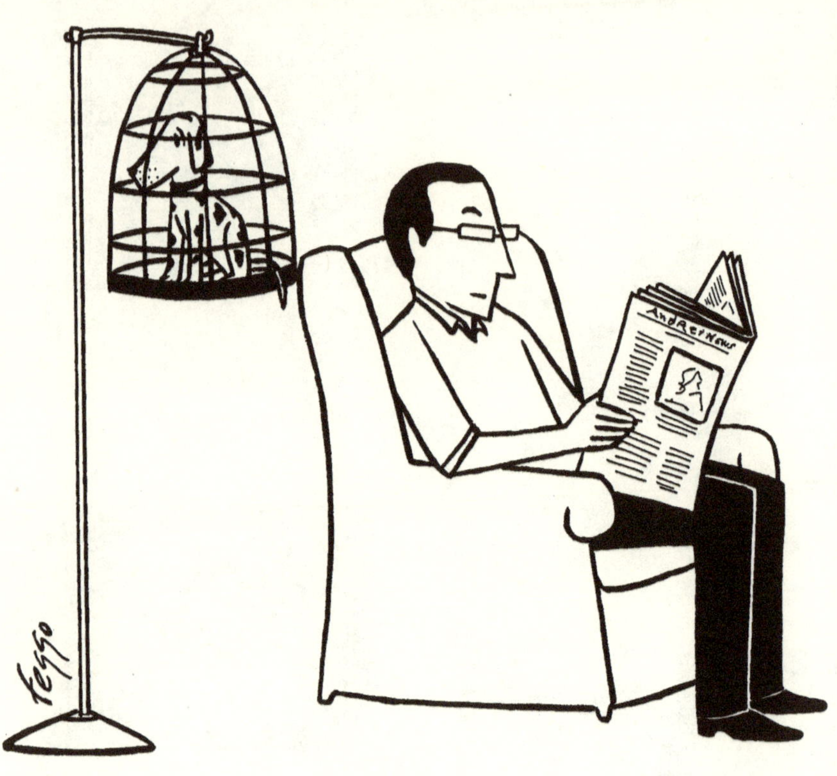
AndReiNews
Feggo

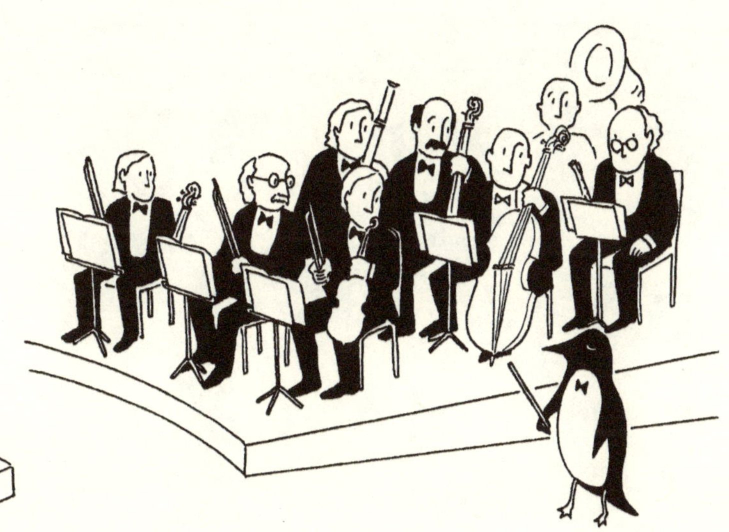
feggo

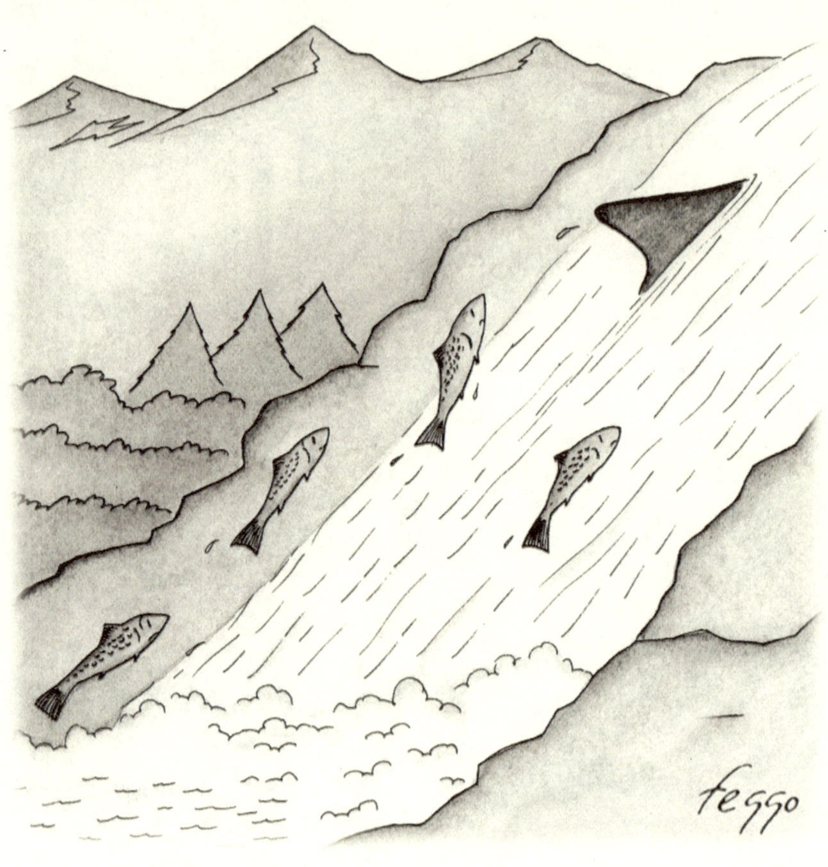
feggo

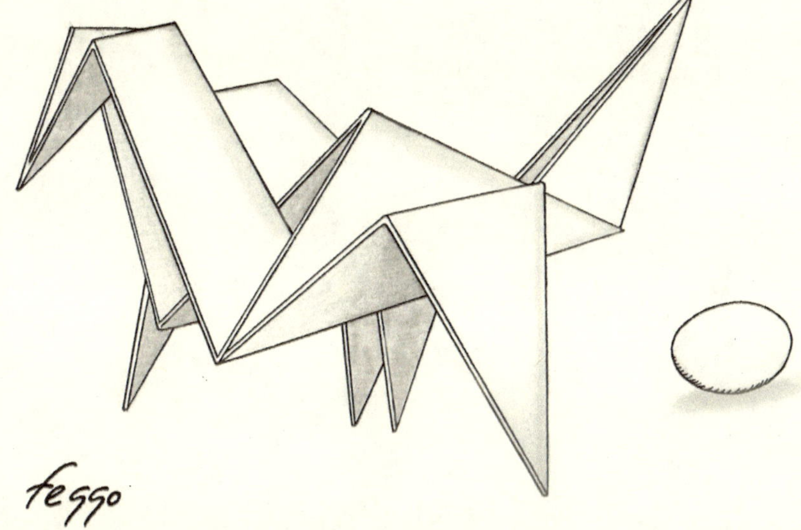
feggo

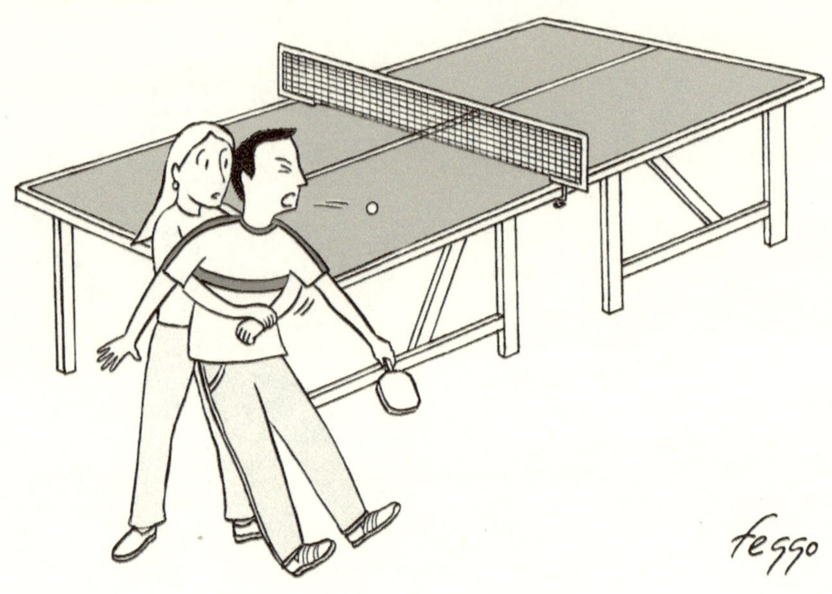
feggo

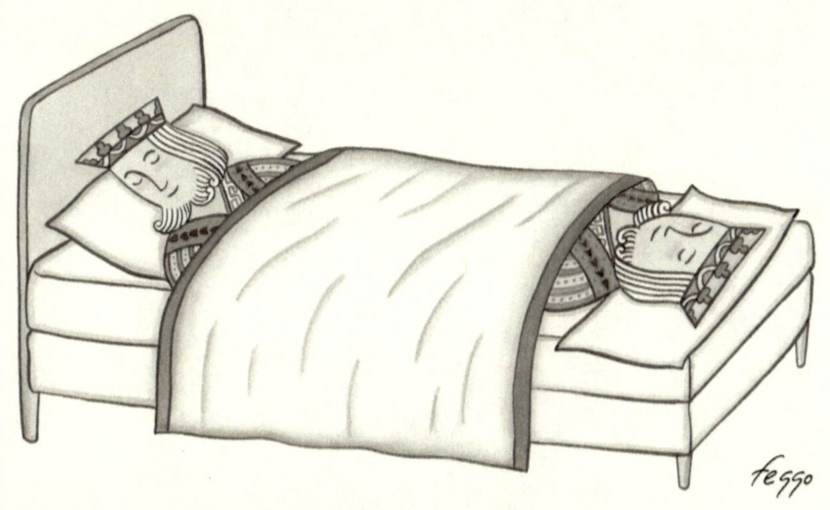
feggo

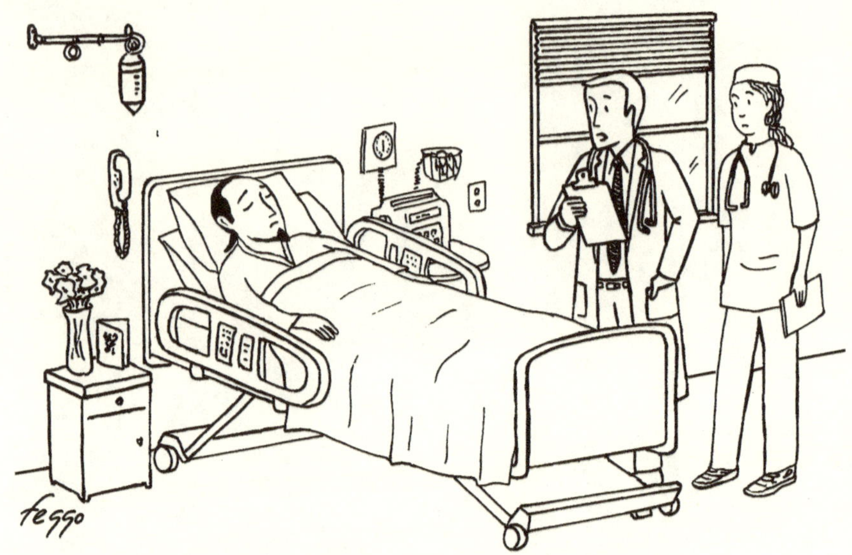

"Critics take a while to die – all their reviewed works flash before their eyes."

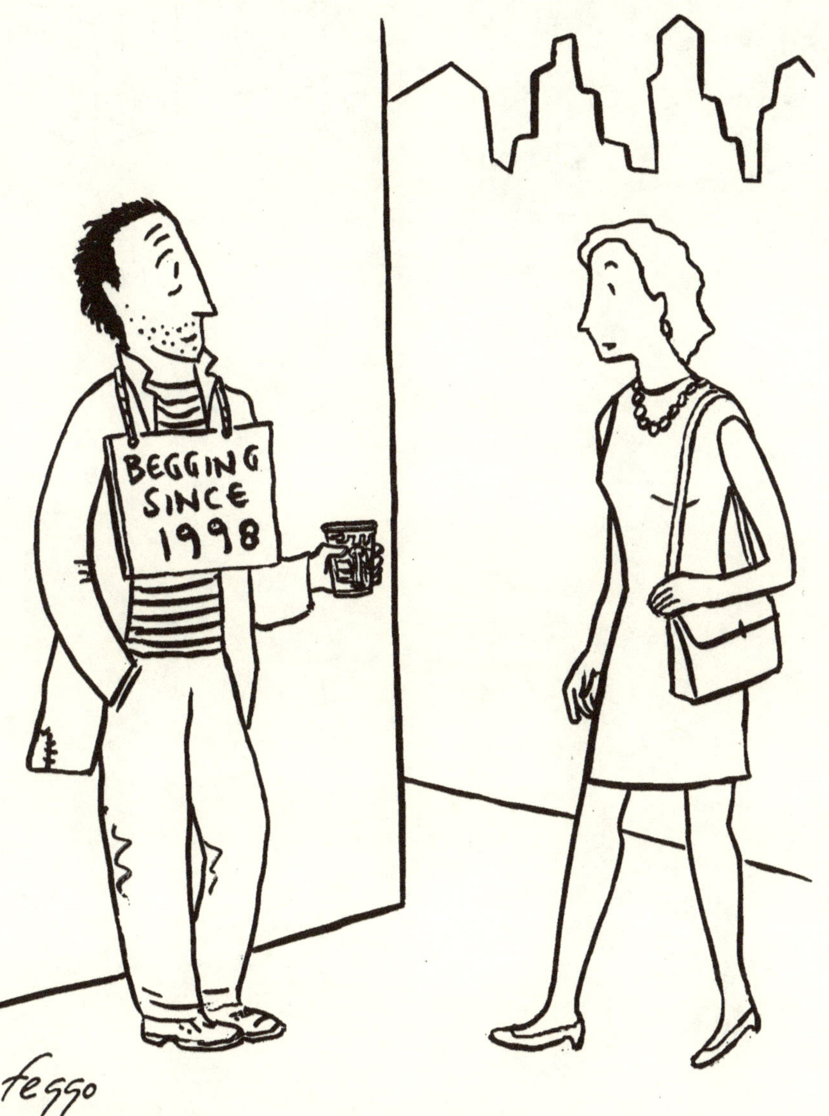
BEGGING
SINCE
1998
feggo

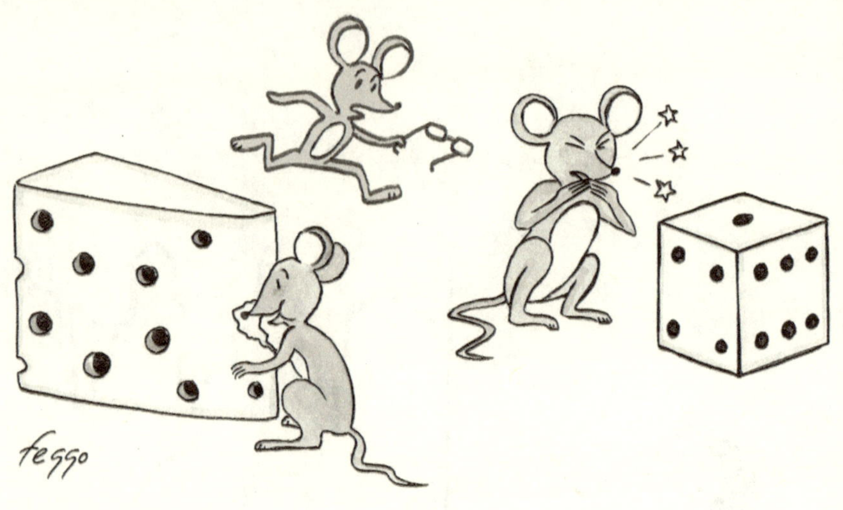
feggo

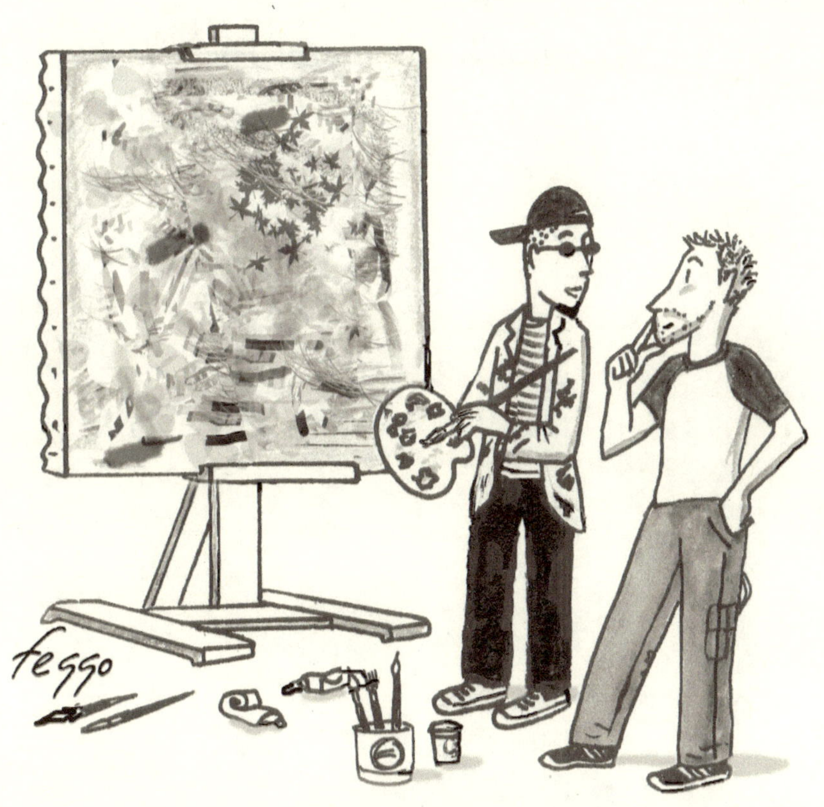

"These days I price my paintings according to the price of oil."

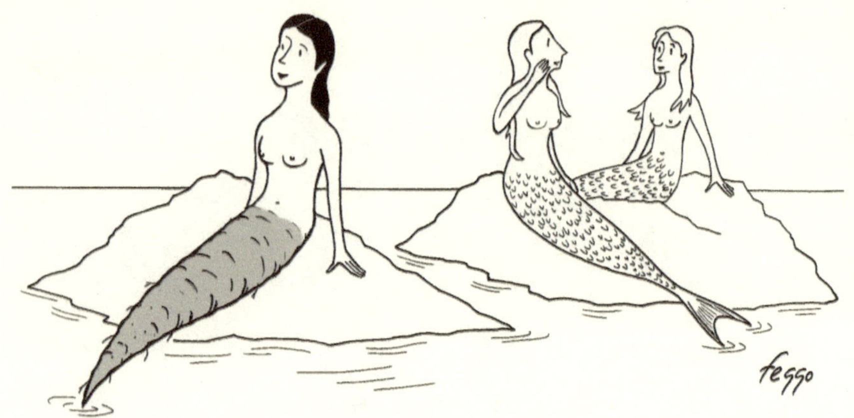

"Her mother was a vegetarian."

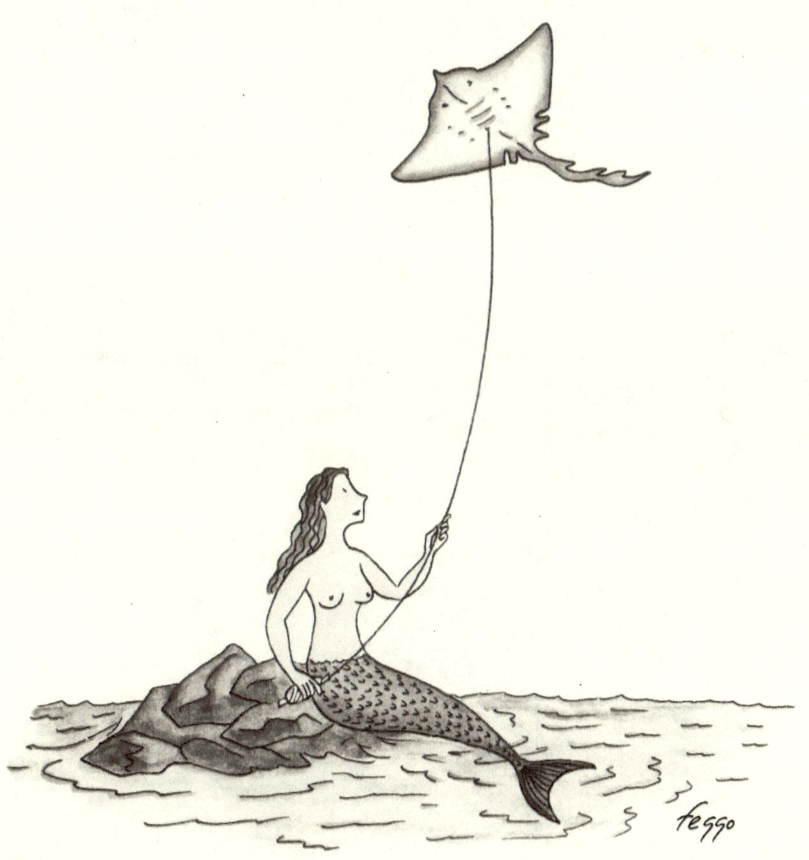
feggo

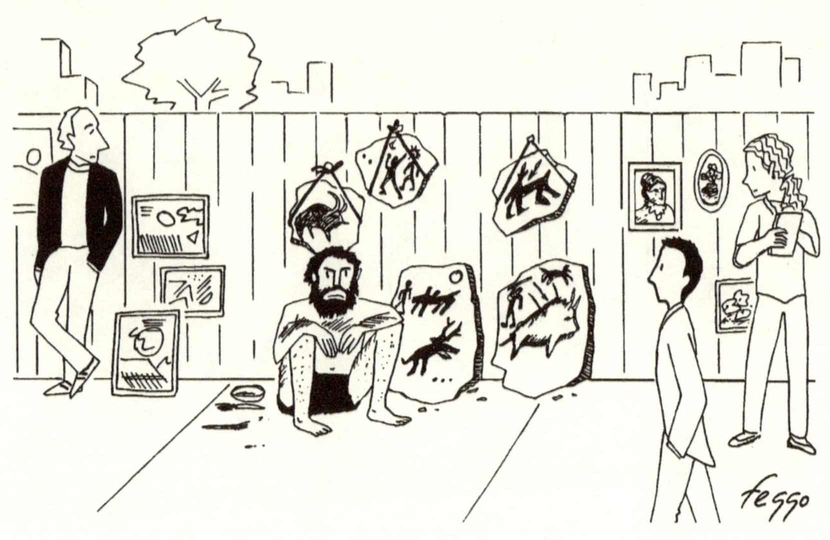

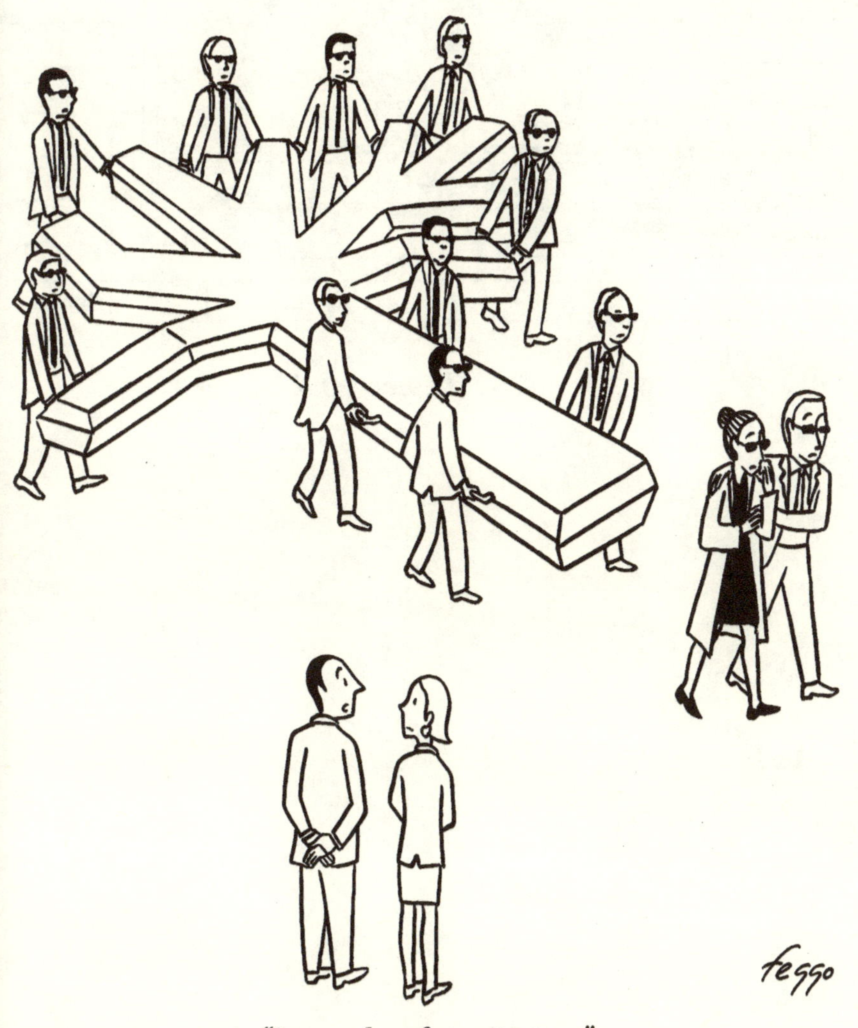

"It was her favorite tree."

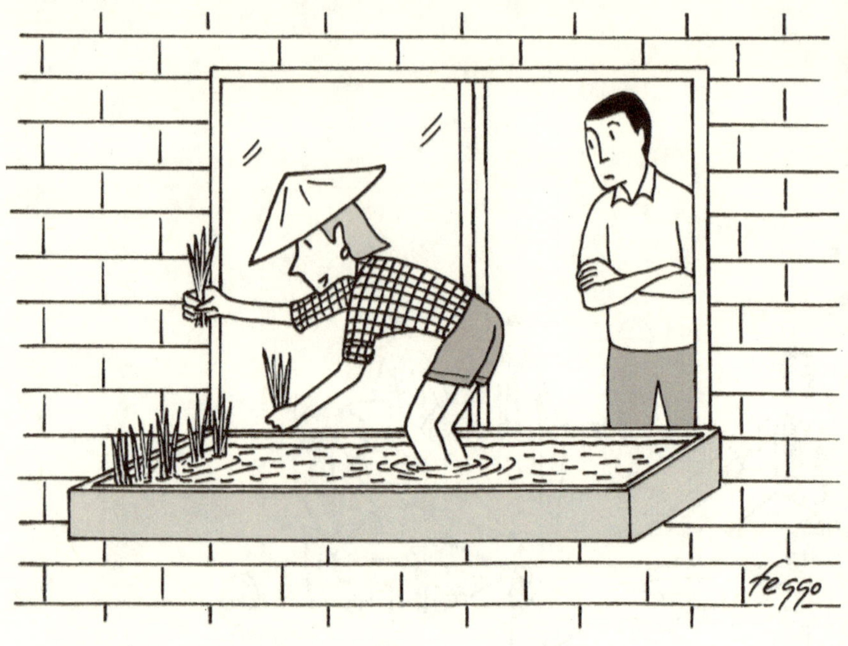

"Rice is the new gold."

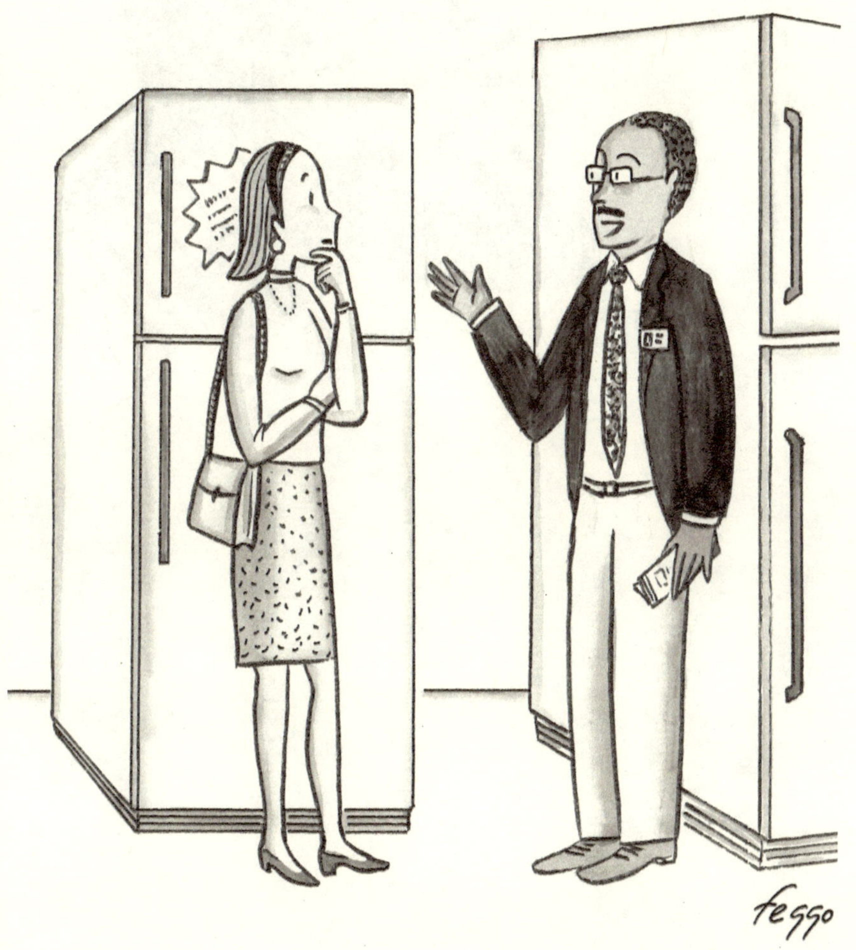

"This model holds at least 75 pictures on its doors."

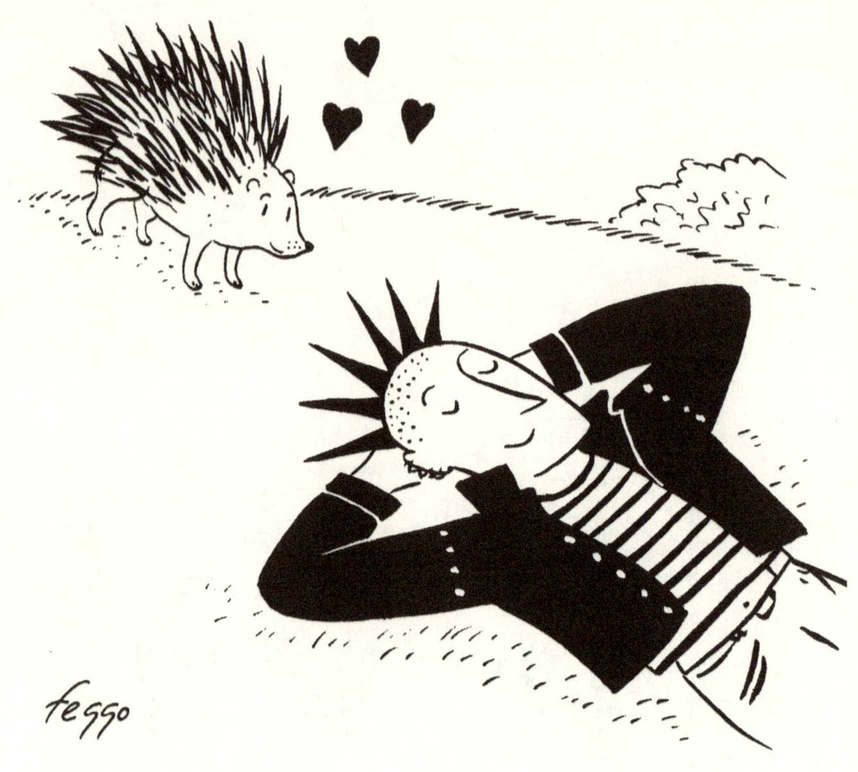
feggo

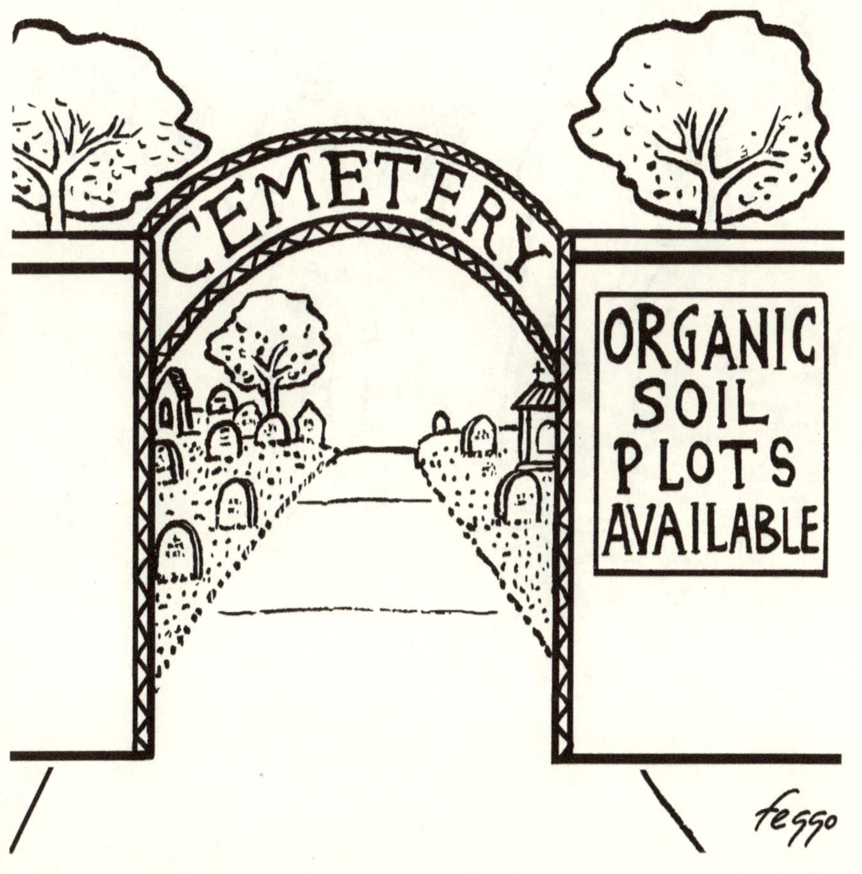
CEMETERY
ORGANIC
SOIL
PLOTS
AVAILABLE
feggo

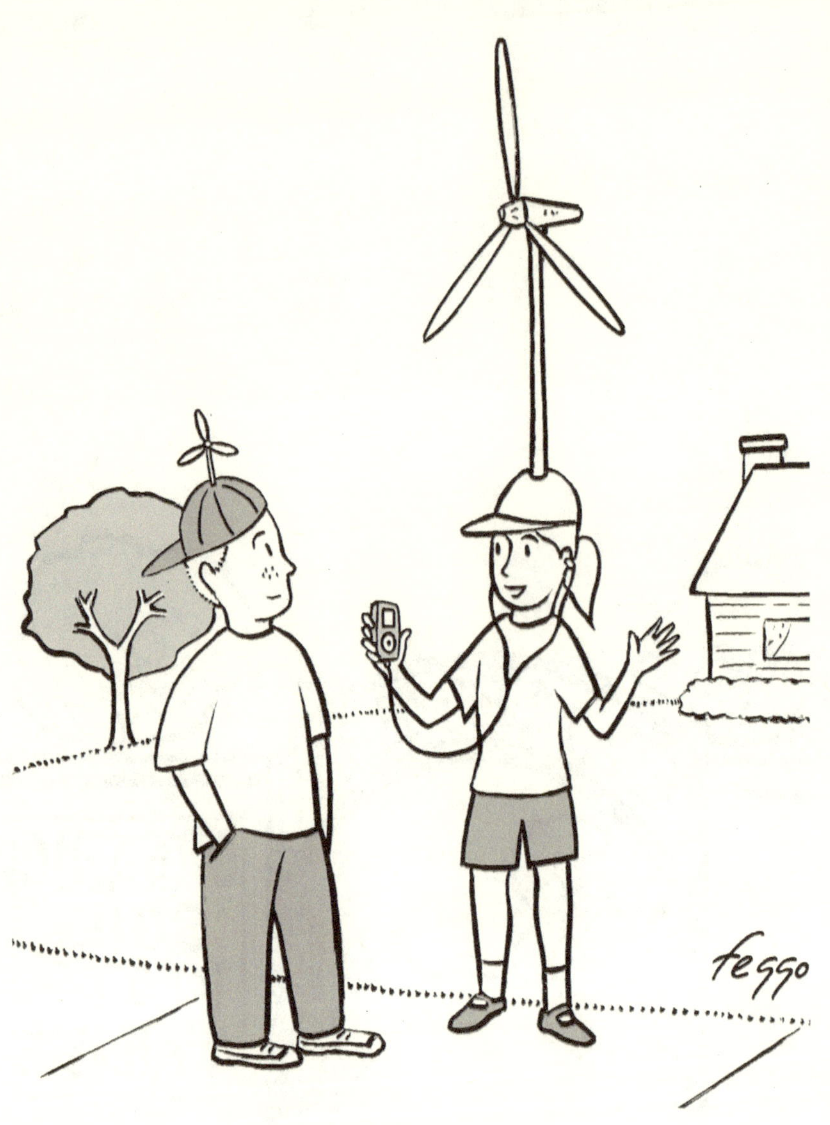

"It recharges my iPod."

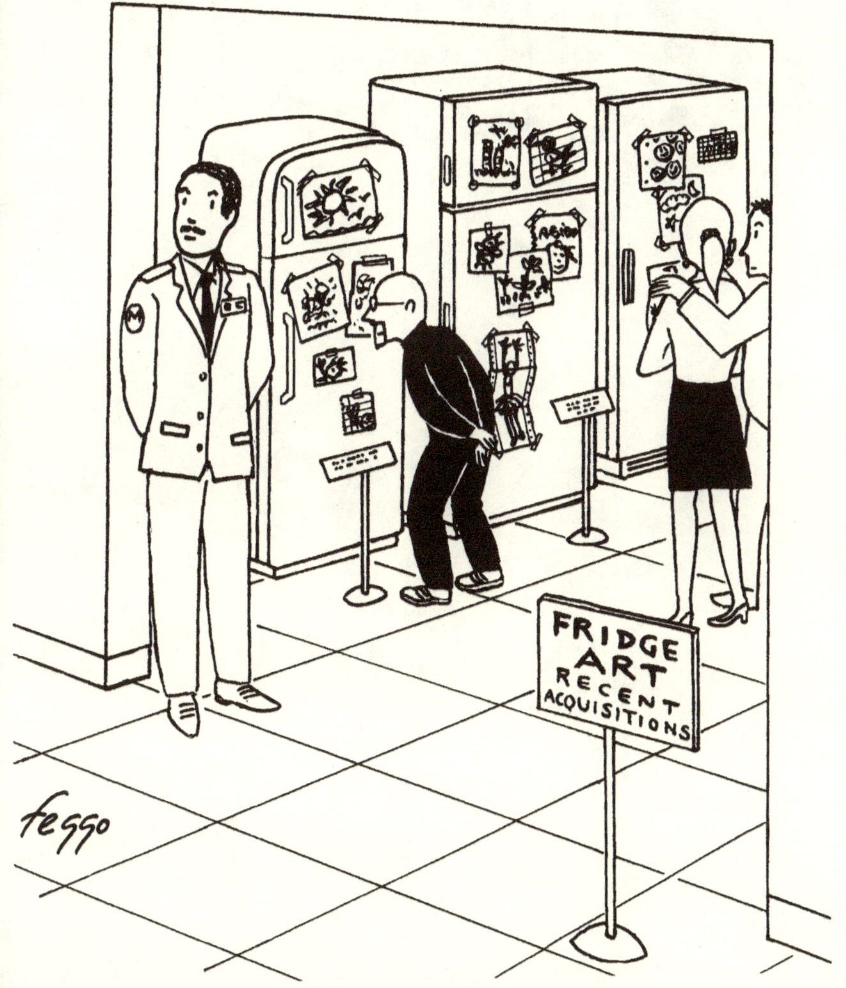
FRIDGE
ART
RECENT
ACQUISITIONS
feggo

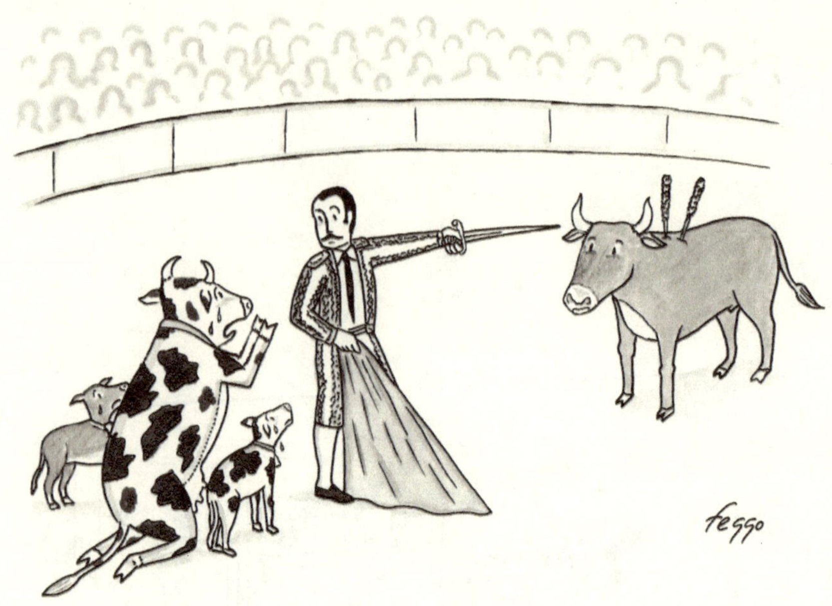
feggo

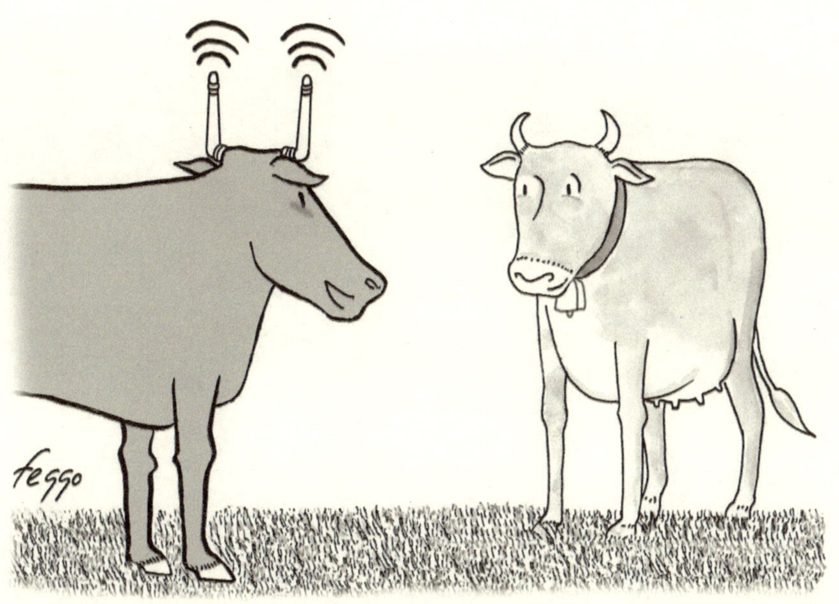

"I just got Wi-Fi."

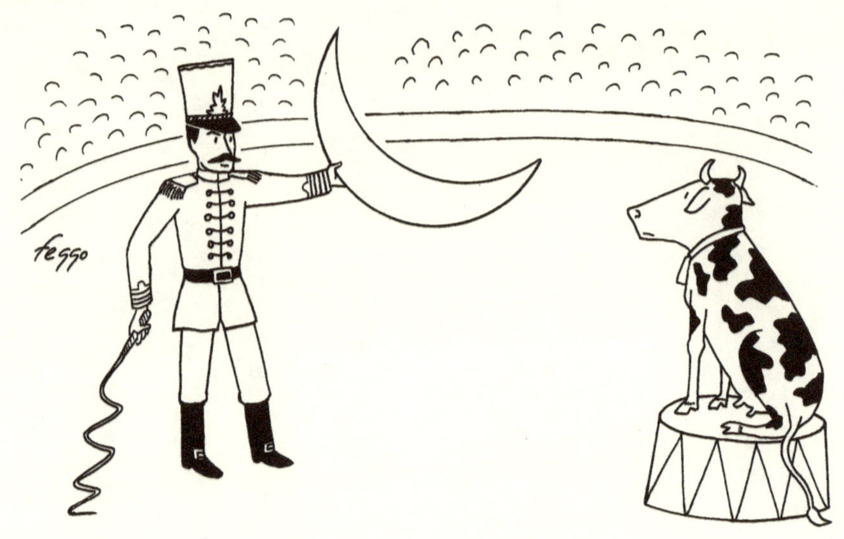
feggo

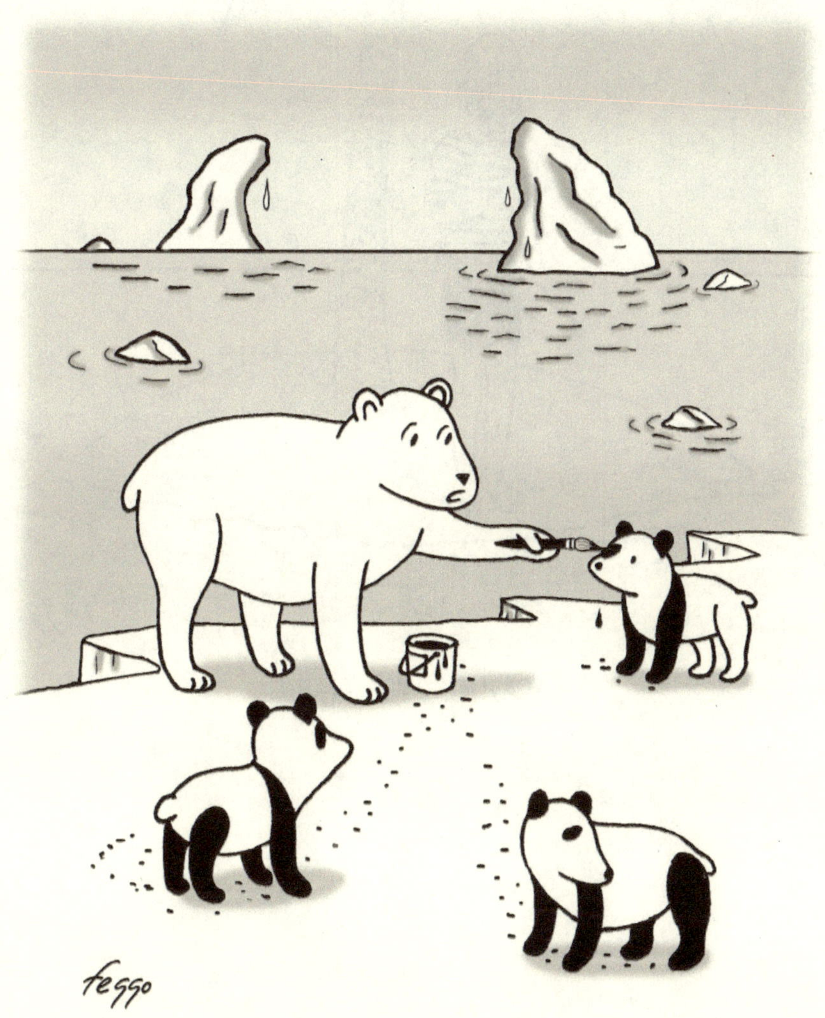

"We can't stay here, and your father has connections in China."

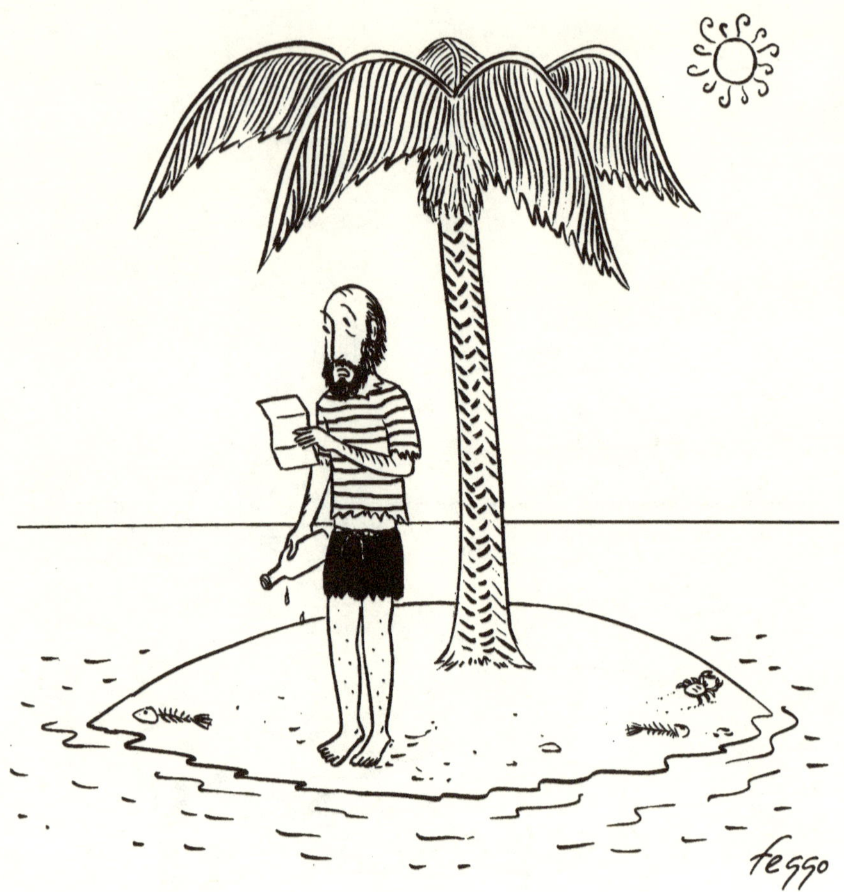

"Not jury duty again!"

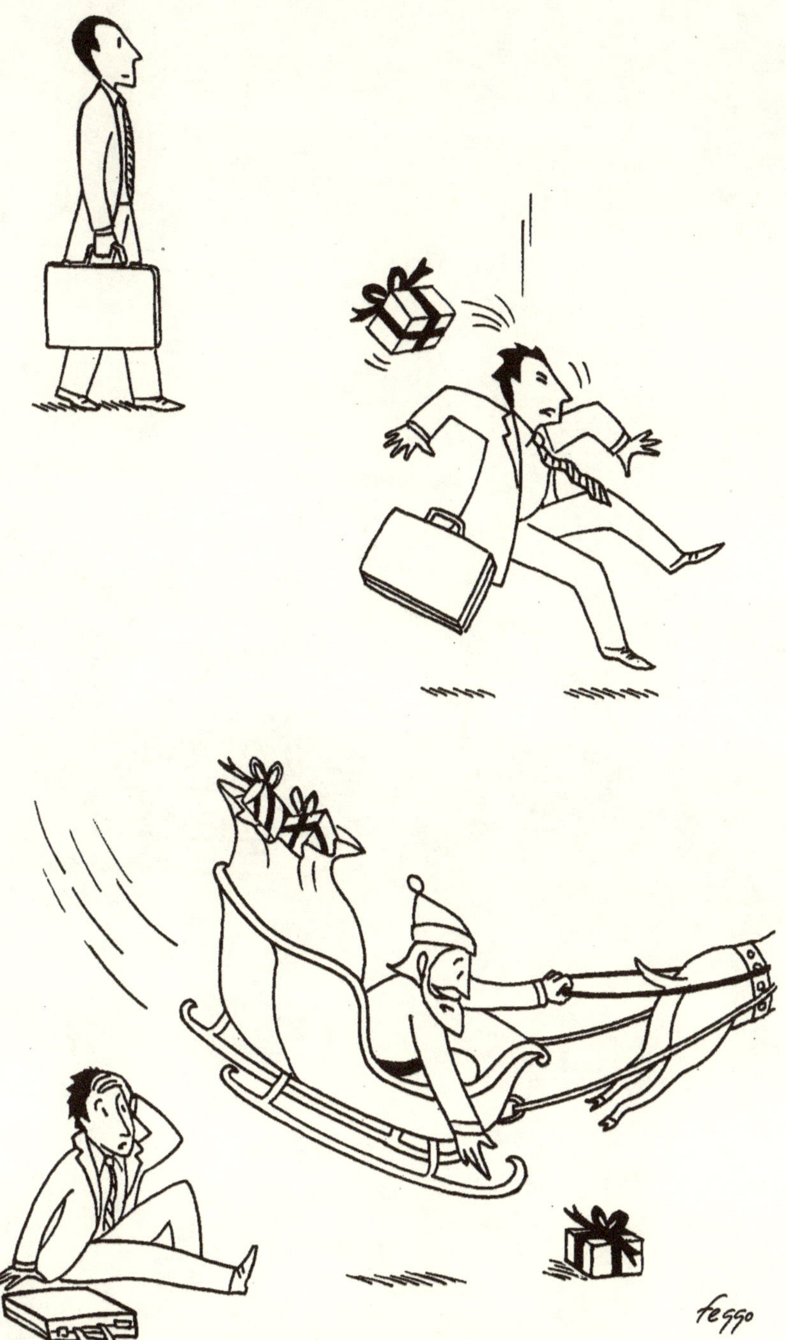
feggo

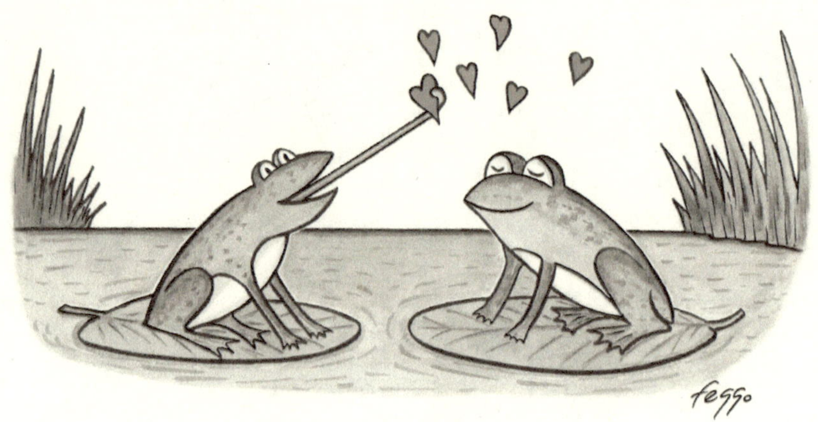
feggo

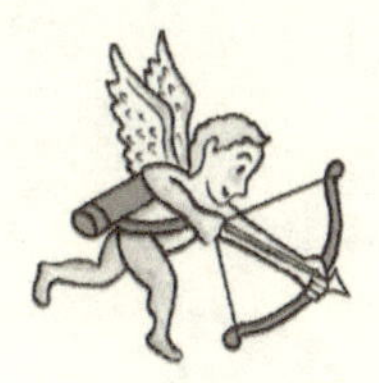

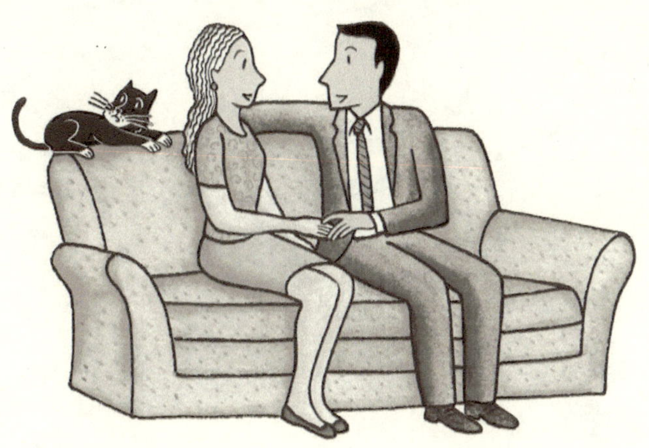

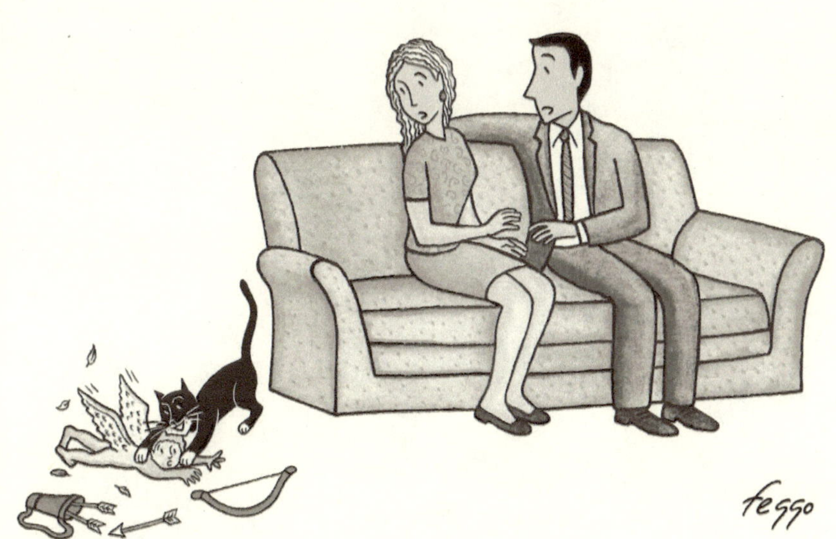
feggo

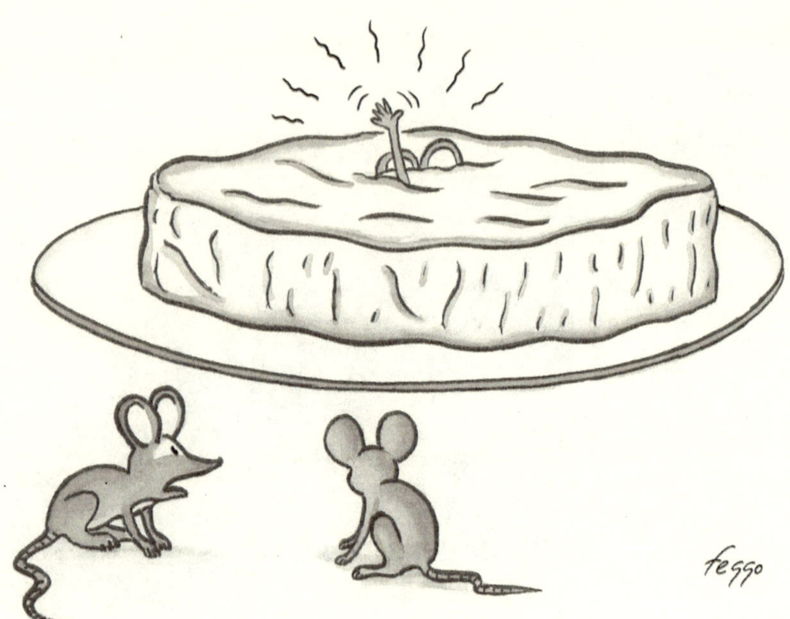

"That's why I avoid Brie."

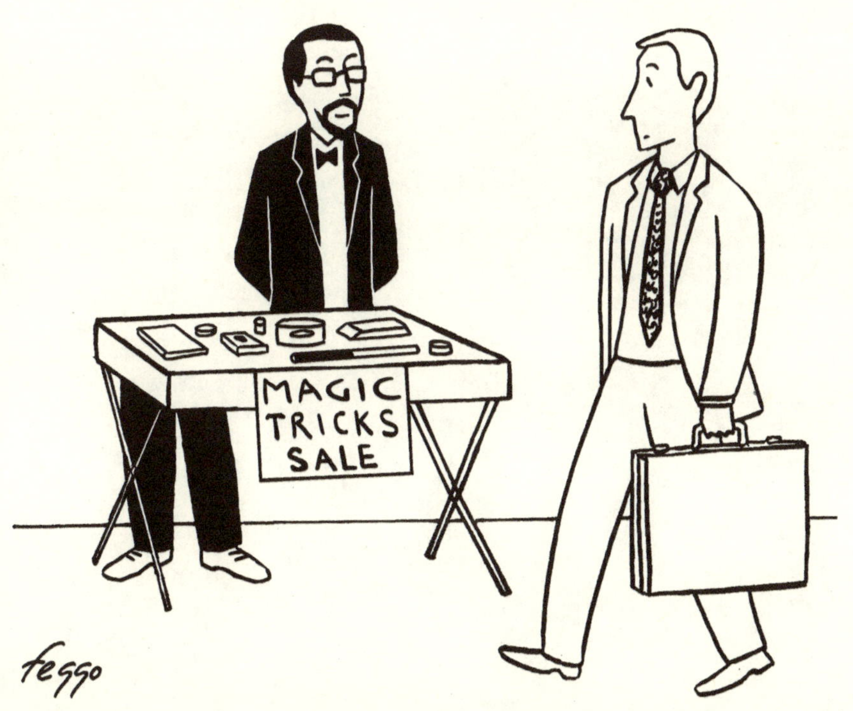
MAGIC
TRICKS
SALE
feggo

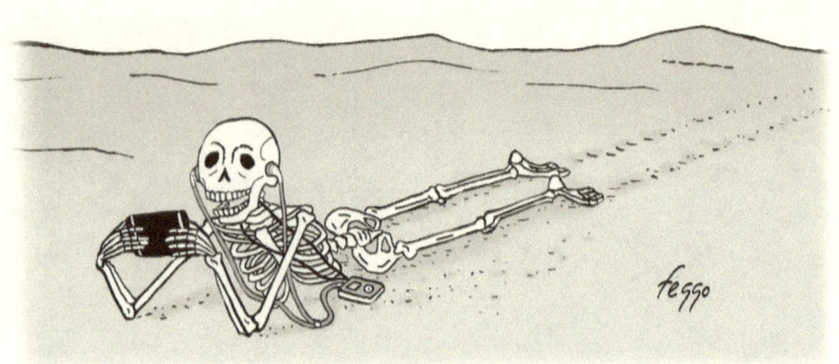
feggo

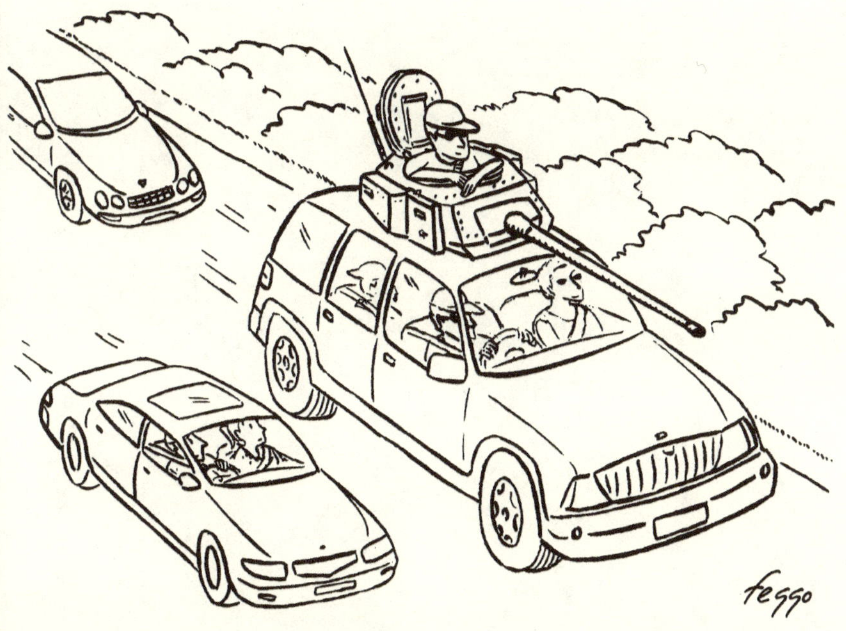
feggo

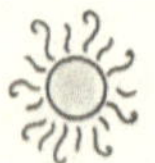

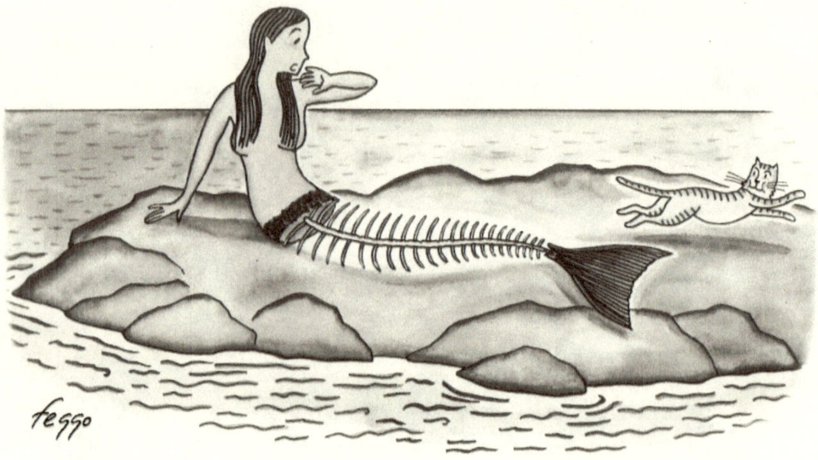
feggo

Acknowledgements

This book is dedicated to my funny muse Andrea.

Muchas Gracias to Sid Harris
for his introductory text and friendly advise
and to my colleague-amigos
Sam Gross, Gahan Wilson, Marissa Acocella-Marchetto,
Jack Ziegler and Bob Mankoff.

Grateful acknowledgements are made to:
Norman Hotz, Michael Heath, Richard Ingrams, Pam Budz,
Kim Rylander, Chris Curry, Markus Nowak, Brenda Leensvaart,
Francesca Messina, Lauren Spitzer, Tony Rushton,
Susha Lee-Shothaman, Chris Duffy, Sam Viviano, Ryan Flanders,
Jonathan Bresman, Aris Malandrakis, Monika Kind, Joshua Clark,
Hans Suter, Horst Rasch, Doug Hunt, Larry Wood, Bob Razinger,
Peter Schleger, Ron L. Gunczler, Michaela Hamilton, Martin Kozlowski,
T.E.D. Klein, Margarita García Flores, Héctor Aguilar Camín,
Rafael Pérez Gay, Magú, Rius
and to absent friends: Roxanna Sayre, Chris Howland,
Jürgen Sparh (Jüsp) and Jerry Robinson.

These cartoons originally appeared in the following publications:
The New Yorker, Reader's Digest, Barron's, The Wall Street Journal,
Mad, Mad Kids, Nickelodeon, Narrative, National Lampoon,
Omni, Audubon, The New York Times, Woman's World, First,
The National Law Journal, Ad Age, American Health, Twilight Zone
and in the international publications:
Private Eye, The Spectator, The Oldie, Prospect (England),
Nebelspalter, Schweizer Illustrierte (Switzerland), *F1 Red Bulletin* (Austria),
Haüser, Playboy (Germany), *Ode* (Netherlands), *Para Pente* (Greece),
Il Guerin Sportivo (Italy),
Los Universitarios, Nexos, La Jornada (Mexico.)

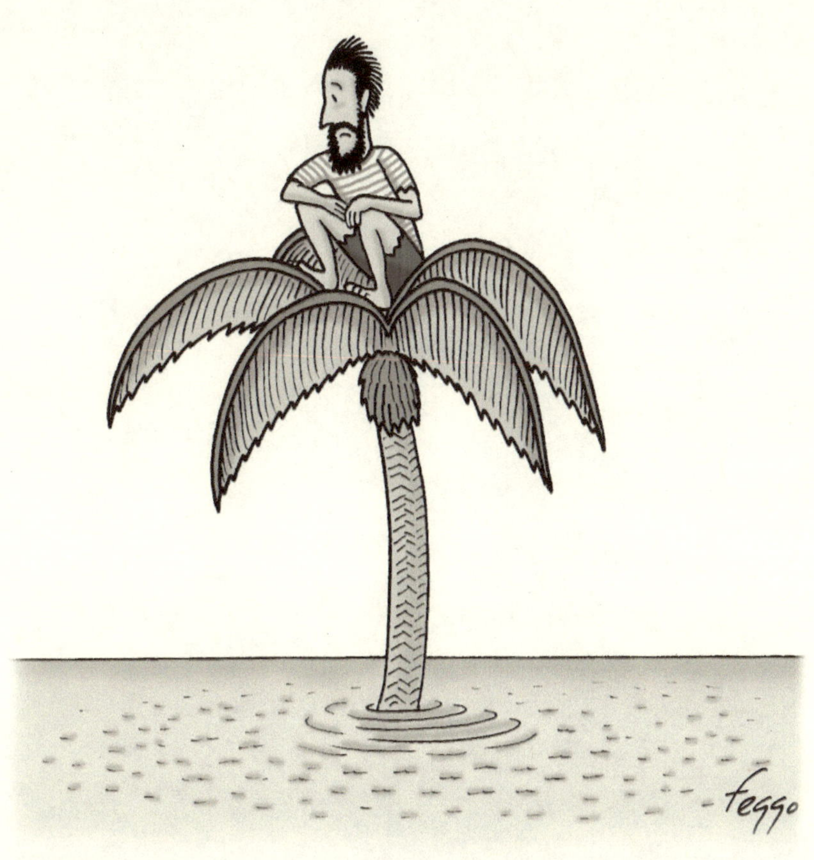

THE FUTURE OF THE DESERT ISLAND

www.ingramcontent.com/pod-product-compliance
Lightning Source LLC
LaVergne TN
LVHW090956080826
845145LV00003B/1030

* 9 7 8 1 9 3 4 9 7 8 6 9 6 *